To GARY -

Keep CARING
& SHARING -

GOD Bless -
Jim
'94

The Joy of Inspired Teaching

Also by Tim Lautzenheiser:

The Art of Successful Teaching:
A Blend of Context and Content

G-4041

The Joy of Inspired Teaching

Tim Lautzenheiser

GIA Publications, Inc.

Library of Congress Cataloging-in-Publication Data

Lautzenheiser, Tim.
    The joy of inspired teaching/Tim Lautzenheiser.
        p. cm.
    "G-4041."
    ISBN 0-941050-50-5 : $19.95
    1. School music—Instruction and study. 2. Teaching. I. Title.
MT1.L393 1993
780′.7—dc20   93–39385
                                                                                                        CIP
                                                                                                        MN

Portions of this book have appeared in slightly different form in the following publications:
Bandworld, TME, The Woman Conductor, Lablanc Bell, International Association of Jazz
Educators Journal and the book Life in the Music Classroom published by the Music Educators
National Conference.

Contents

Foreword
by Dr. William D. Revelli

W elcome to *The Joy of Inspired Teaching* by Tim Lautzenheiser. You are destined to feel a sense of joy and inspiration as you read through the chapters of this wonderful book. The title aptly describes the positive effect Tim's thoughts will have on every person involved in teaching.

I have had the opportunity to work with Tim on several occasions and am proud to call him one of my dearest friends. He is a very talented musician both as a performer and a conductor (and I happen to know that he loves to spend time on the podium and in the classroom), but he has chosen to dedicate his life to working with an often-forgotten, but most essential, facet of music: the quest for excellence and the personal attitude needed to attain it. I don't know of anyone who has done more in developing this area of music education, and his contributions should be embraced by every teacher in our schools.

It would be impossible to read this fine book and not be inspired about teaching music. Tim encourages us to get beyond the minor inconveniences that we face in our daily schedule and to reach into our hearts and souls to remember why we chose to be teachers in the first place. It is a very healthy perspective and serves as a strong reminder of our responsibilities to always give our students a quality learning experience. His honesty is refreshing, his style is invigorating, and his message is profound.

Although I do not have many regrets in life, I have often told Tim I am sorry he was not a part of one of my bands at the University of Michigan. However, he has been a loyal student throughout our friendship and it is a special honor for me to introduce you to his latest writing. Undoubtedly this is only one of many books to come from Tim's pen, but I can assure you that this one will become a classic in every educator's library, as it should be.

It is a privilege to welcome you to *The Joy of Inspired Teaching* and the wisdom of Tim Lautzenheiser.

ABOUT DR. WILLIAM D. REVELLI

If there ever was an individual who epitomizes *The Joy of Inspired Teaching*, it is Dr. William D. Revelli. The impact this man has had on the field of music education is nothing short of remarkable. He is the lifetime Chairman of the Board in our profession.

Over the years, I have enjoyed many occasions working alongside Dr. Revelli, and through this association I have acquired an education that could not be measured in terms of tuition. He is a master teacher, and simply being in his presence confirms that teaching is an art form. His passion for music is second only to his personal commitment of sharing it with everyone he meets.

Life has brought many blessings my way, and the friendship and mentorship of Dr. Revelli stands as one of my most cherished gifts. There has never been a time when he wasn't ready and willing to offer his help, his guidance, and his wisdom. It is an honor and a privilege to include his supportive thoughts as the foreword to *The Joy of Inspired Teaching*.

Introduction
by Michael Kumer

"For the demand for change in the thought pattern may engender the feeling that the ground is to be pulled from under one's feet."
—Werner Karl Heisenberg

Werner Heisenberg's comment about the revolution in early twentieth-century physics applies as readily to the quieter contemporary evolution in education. Information concerning best teaching practices is unsurpassed due to the avalanche of books, articles, videos, and other media. Why then the resistance to incorporate what we know into what we do? And, more importantly, what can be done to turn the *burden* of change into the *opportunity* for intellectual, emotional, and spiritual growth?

. Answers to these questions form the keystone of Tim Lautzenheiser's magnificent new book, *The Joy of Inspired Teaching*, in which a trusted guide illuminates a pathway to understanding, appreciation, and action. Tim has long embraced the notion that music education is among the most noble professions precisely because of its potential to widen the boundaries of the human experience. In his book, Tim supports the realization of this potential by contributing an eloquent review of core pedagogical values as well as an insightful set of strategies for elevating encounters with students into treasured moments.

The Joy of Inspired Teaching encourages our belief that change and challenge are desirable, perhaps inevitable characteristics, the presence of which propels us on a satisfying journey through life. And during that journey, as compellingly suggested by Tim Lautzenheiser, it is the strength of our convictions that steadies the ground under our feet.

ABOUT MICHAEL KUMER

Michael Kumer, Dean of the School of Music at Duquesne University in Pittsburgh, has been a lifelong friend and confidant. He is a devoted student of positive potential, and his own professional success is an affirmation that he *walks his talk*. He is pro-active, open-minded, intuitively sensitive, and has the innate ability to say exactly the right thing at the right time. He is a leader of leaders.

While many were ambivalent (and even discouraging) about my decision to become an independent advocate for music education, Michael was eagerly fueling the vision with his personal encouragement and enthusiastic suggestions. To this day, when I find myself starting to give in to negative influence, I immediately call Michael, and he quickly puts everything into perspective, reminds me of the need to give up giving up, and gently but firmly pushes me back in the performance of life. A friend/partner/brother of that caliber is priceless.

Thank you, Michael, for your meaningful words and for contributing in more ways than you can possibly imagine to *The Joy of Inspired Teaching*.

"We don't see the world as it is, but we see the world as we are."

Thoughts about Reading This Book

To read *The Joy of Inspired Teaching* is not going to transform anyone's life, nor should it. What this book may do is stimulate your thinking, provoke some fresh ideas, or even bring a smile to your face. If so: mission accomplished.

The Joy of Inspired Teaching is not meant to stand alongside the typical textbook or research project; quite the contrary. This book is meant for those moments when you want to be encouraged or are tired of being discouraged. Most certainly, there is nothing to be found in these pages that will change the course of mankind or even alter your own plans for tomorrow, but this book may help you see what a valuable role you play in the education of a child.

Please don't try to read it from beginning to end. You will be sorely disappointed. Each chapter stands alone. There is no relation from one to the other, nor is there intended to be. If you have five minutes and need a bit of a boost, you will probably find something in the table of contents that will be appropriate—choose that particular chapter and go on your merry way.

Most of all, realize that you do make a difference. Your contribution to this world is far more than you can measure.

You bring out the best in your students, and we must continue to offer our young generation the finest programs in music education we can develop. It is an honorable goal. Perhaps you will find some inspiration in this book to help you embrace and perpetuate this important role.

I join you in a personal commitment to our young people. As noted educator George Leonard says, "Our task is to help every child become in his or her own way an artist, to help every child become a genius, and to see just how far toward ecstasy and accomplishment every human being can go." Bravo!

—Tim Lautzenheiser
September 1993

"The longer I live, the more I realize the impact of attitude on life. Attitude to me is more important than facts. It is more important than the past, than education, than money, than circumstances, than failures, than successes, than what other people think or say or do. It is more important than appearance, giftedness, or skill. It will make or break a company...a church...a home. The remarkable thing is you have a choice every day regarding the attitude you will embrace for that day. We cannot change our past...we cannot change the fact that people will act in a certain way. We cannot change the inevitable. The only thing we can do is play on the one string we have, and that is our attitude. I am convinced that life is ten percent what happens to me and ninety percent how I react to it. And so it is with you. You are in charge of your attitude."
—Charles R. Swindoll

Part One

Philosophy of
Music Education

*"People are more persuaded by the depth of your conviction
than by the strength of your logic."*

Philosophy of Music Education

Every now and then we must stop and focus on why we chose to become music teachers. It is so easy to become involved in the doing that we can easily forget the *reason* we are doing in the first place. We must remind ourselves of the importance of our influence on young people, and constantly re-dedicate ourselves to our own philosophical foundation.

Do you remember the requisite assignment for your college class, Music 101: My Philosophy of Music Education? Are you still living that self-imposed credo? Have your thoughts, ideas, visions shifted since then? Has your enthusiasm for teaching music remained at that high level of excitement? Do you still have a passion for the art form? Those can be very uncomfortable questions, and perhaps in your zeal to complete your present assigned teaching agenda, you might want to review that paper you faithfully wrote to fulfill the requirements for Music 101. Are you living your dream?

This particular section of *The Joy of Inspired Teaching* will allow you to look beyond the daily problems and sense the overall importance of music education. It is easy to forget that teaching music is more than preparing for the concert, passing out the audition music, collecting the revenue from the fund-raiser, or ordering the busses for the upcoming trip. Teaching music is about preparing our students to live life. In a school environment where impressionistic learning is revered, you offer a chance for *expressionistic* learning. Music is much more than memorizing data that will be measured by a test. Music is not a matter of choosing answers on a multiple choice examination, but rather, it provides the opportunity to learn an artistic vocabulary to express the creative mind. The challenge is great; the positive benefits are infinite.

As you read the chapters in this section, do not agree or disagree with everything written. Simply allow the thoughts to sift through your own philosophy of music education. Take advantage of what supports your direction and simply dismiss what does not. This is a chance to be boldly reminded of what a vital role you play in creating a *path for success* for your students. It might even cause you to dig through you archives and pull out that assignment from Music 101!

"Pleasure is a shadow, wealth is vanity, and power a pageant; but knowledge is ecstatic in enjoyment, perennial in frame, unlimited in space, and infinite in duration."
—*DeWitt Clinton*

A Rewarding Lifetime Goal

Another school year is in progress, and for every music educator, excellence is at the forefront of the curricular agenda, as it should be. Regardless of the approach, everyone is committed to creating a positive experience for the students who choose to be a part of the music program. Given that, let us look at the issue of *intrinsic* vs. *extrinsic* motivation on this important path to success.

So much of our society is based on *product* rather than *process*. Instant gratification has led to fast foods, microwave meals, one-hour cleaners, overnight mail, and tanning lotions which guarantee a full bronze exterior in just a few short minutes without the burden of going outside in the sun. For our young music enthusiasts, it is much easier to put on the CD headphones and listen to a recording than it is to drag out the instrument and diligently practice the major and minor scales.

In an effort to motivate the beginning musician, it is often tempting to add some outside benefits, i.e. "Every student who learns all the scales by the end of the first six weeks will receive a free T-shirt." For some, that will offer the necessary incentive to take the time to spend an hour each day with instrument in hand. The success of their personal discipline will be rewarded with a symbol of achievement, the shirt. However, it is important everyone involved in this procedure understand the *reward* is different than the *goal.* The goal is to learn the scales. The reward is the T-shirt.

With the ongoing and heated dialog concerning the controversy of musical competition, ratings and rankings, adjudication procedures, etc., we must all make a clear distinction in our profession: the goal is to teach the understanding and appreciation of music, the reward comes via the accolades along the way. *The goals are intrinsic. The rewards are extrinsic. Music is intrinsic; therefore, the goals are far more significant than the rewards.*

To avoid extrinsic motivation is next to impossible in our culture. We are given a paycheck for our teaching efforts. It represents a reward for a job well done; but if our goal is the revenue, then teaching is only a means to the end. Certainly, the financial aspect of any profession is necessary to maintain a lifestyle, but hopefully the goal is the intrinsic joy of sharing the knowledge of music. In most situations one could not enjoy the *process* of the goal without the *product* of the reward. This symbiotic structure has kept outstanding educators in the profession. If money was the goal, there would be very few teachers in the classroom.

Extrinsic rewards are effective in short-term situations, but if they become the substitute for intrinsic goals, then we are on a certain collision course with the results being a loss of the student's interest and eventually the loss of the student. In blunt terms, they quit. They simply become tired of chasing the proverbial carrot and turn in their instrument for something more enticing. However, if they are exposed to the intrinsic goals of music education, they will find personal pleasure in practice and performance and will embrace music as an integral part of life.

It is all too easy to make ratings and rankings the end-all measure of quality. It can be tempting to delude students, parents, administrators, and ourselves into thinking a first-place trophy represents effective teaching. (And this is not to say that getting a high rating does not indicate good teaching.) Everyone enjoys such an uplifting award, but the real measure of success comes from the process of learning which took place in preparation for the rewarding performance; therein lies the attainment of the *goal*. When the discipline of personal growth is the focus of the rehearsals, the students will see music as a language of individual expression rather than a sport of measured achievement. When that transition is in place, they become faithful participants and consumers for a lifetime—and we have become teachers who brought them an art which will afford a new level of understanding in every facet of their future. *Mission accomplished*...the mission of music education.

It is apparent that one of our top priorities must be to keep the students involved in the music program; otherwise, there is little hope they will continue their relationship with music. Recruitment plays a vital role in the growth and development of the ensembles, but retention is equally important, for it is at the intermediate and advanced levels of technique development that the goals are realized and the joy of music becomes a personal pleasure beyond words, only to be described by the music itself.

Yes, it is exciting and rewarding to feel the accomplishments of a successful adjudication experience, but it is far more fulfilling and worthwhile to put one's heart into a performance and feel the intrinsic satisfaction only music can bring to the human soul.

"Before enlightenment, chop wood, carry water.
After enlightenment, chop wood, carry water."

Success in Music Education: Chop Wood, Carry Water

What does it take to get our students to achieve a high level of musical proficiency? When do we get to the point where we don't have to repeat the same instructions over and over until we are blue in the face, only to have several people still not grasp the information? Will the seniors ever quit graduating just as they start to blossom into talented performers? It's like painting the Brooklyn Bridge: By the time we finish one end, the other end is ready for the proverbial paint brush of life. Will it ever end?

In building a successful program, the theme of *musical excellence* is the primary foundation block. It is impossible to have a quality performance without skilled musicians. Students may often be talented, but lack the fundamental knowledge about how to express their talents in an artistic manner. Music education is a basic necessity to achieve this goal. Most certainly, there are a few innately gifted people who will become outstanding musicians outside the system, but most are dependent on our school curricula to serve as their vehicle to the enjoyment of music and the intrinsic pleasure it brings to life. Without our school music classes, many young people will never have this important option in their formative years, let alone in their adult life.

Without you, the music teacher, they are somewhat at the whim of a musical diet consisting of Top-40 hits, the latest MTV release, and the hottest CD on the charts. (There could well be some merit to any and all of these, but other options should also be added to this musical meal.) Your influence is wanted and needed.

Perhaps we cannot save the masses, or educate every person about the genius of Mozart, Brahms, Beethoven, Wagner, Gershwin, etc., but we can influence the young ladies and gentlemen who walk into our classrooms each day. We do have control over their musical destiny and can make sure they are exposed to the pillars of our musical heritage as well as the most contemporary creations of our time. What's more, it seems as though that should be our valued credo: *to bring the very best music to their learning experience.*

The appreciation of good music is often a developed taste. It requires a personal understanding of many aspects of the composition, performance, history, theory, composer's background, etc. The beauty of the sonorities is only one facet of the overall comprehension of a piece of music. We need to be made aware of all the other aspects of the whys and wherefores of the piece so we can relate it to the various parts of our lives. When this is done, we are in store for a quality experience at the highest level of human understanding. However, for this to happen, we need devoted music educators who are enthusiastic about leading young people along the journey of musical awareness: true music education.

Every knowledgeable teacher of music is agreeing with the above thoughts, but may be asking, "What's the point?" *We all know where we should be going,* the difficulty is in *getting there.* Musical utopia is much like a moving target, and the closer we get to it, the faster it moves. What is the certain route to ensure that our students will *arrive?* Is it a particular curriculum, a certain teaching method, a foolproof system, programing a specific list of compositions? What will guarantee our students the most positive and successful music education they will carry on throughout their lives?

Chop wood, carry water!

Before you run for an ax and a bucket, finish this essay; it might save you from cutting your finger and drenching your shoes. This essay is about integrating a concept into your style of teaching, and this concept will fit any and all styles. It might be labeled *persistence, tenacity, perseverance, fortitude, steadfastness,* etc. It is the inner knowledge that we must never think there is a quick back route to our musical goals. There is a reason the finest professionals continue to work on the basics. They warm up with the kind of intensity that we asked of our own students in every beginning class. They have not forgotten the importance of doing the right thing and doing it the right way. Many have achieved expert status in their given discipline, yet are dedicated students of the basics. The most successful have developed working habits based on proven techniques, not some quick-fix routine. There is a dedication to these basics and a commitment to seeing them through to the end—no excuses, no substitutes, and no side-stepping. In the profession we call it *practicing.* There is no magic pill one can take to gain musical expertise; it is a matter of putting in the time, focusing on the tried-and-true techniques, and realizing this is a lifelong pattern. There is no substitute. Even personal financial wealth cannot replace time on task. One cannot pay someone else to do one's own practicing!

So often, students will have a very successful performance and then fall into a musical slump. The next concert might be six weeks away and festival season might be over. There is not an immediate extrinsic goal, so the temptation to simply "shelve it" for a few days is extremely strong. But during that time we don't just put our musical growth on hold—it's not that forward momentum ceases; rather, it starts to slip backwards. The instrumentalist who puts his or her horn away over the summer knows the frustration and anguish of trying to develop a good sound after a three-month void of practice. Of course, we do not go all the way back to the beginning, but we have to re-establish those important fundamental habits all over. Would it not be more beneficial to simply put in a few minutes each day and continue to improve? Who are we cheating when we don't? (There is no wood in the furnace and no water in the sink! We must continue to chop wood and carry water.)

In a world where we are obsessed with getting things done quickly, the study of music requires just the opposite process. It jealously demands time, figuratively and literally. Music is about using our time, and time is the required payment for being a proficient musician. There is no shortcut, and to assume there might be is just a *waste of time.* Enlightenment in music education is the realization that we must spend countless hours mastering the fundamentals; only then will we enjoy the fruits of our labor in this important art. This process of maturation takes *time.* As music teachers, our own persistence is a necessary component in this success formula. We can never give up on the students and risk losing them in our impatience, for if they are no longer in our classroom, how can we teach them music? We are their stewards, their couriers, their all-important mentors of music, and it is our charge to keep them at our side until we proudly promote them to the next leg of their journey.

Every time you want to throw in the towel, become exasperated because of some schedule conflict, or think you are not appreciated by anyone in the system, simply stop and remember this important bit of wisdom:

Before enlightenment, chop wood, carry water.

After enlightenment, chop wood, carry water.

And so it is...and so it will be.

"Don't evaluate your life in terms of achievements, trivial or monumental, along the way. If you do, you will be destined to the frustration of always seeking out others' destinations, and never allowing yourself actually to be fulfilled. Instead, wake up and appreciate everything you encounter along the path. Enjoy the flowers that are there for your pleasure. Tune in to the sunrise, the little children, the laughter, the rain, and the birds. Drink it all in...there is no way to happiness, happiness is the way."
—Wayne Dyer

The Question Is the Answer

Every music educator is looking for the answer. In fact, not only the answer, but a list of answers which will guarantee musical utopia. If we could only discover the answers to:

- What is the best method for the beginners?
- Which instruments will insure accurate intonation?
- Why doesn't my administration understand my plight?
- Where do we find competent private teachers? And how do we convince students to sign up for them?
- Is there any solid proven recruiting program? Can it offer a solution to balanced instrumentation?
- How do we stop the attrition from middle school to high school?
- How do I get my students to understand the need for a higher level of commitment?

- What music can offer the best growth-experience for a group with an extreme variation in abilities?
- When will the parents realize how important music is?
- Where is the audience? Why doesn't the audience under stand concert etiquette?
- Why can't we have our own computer? How does this computer work? Can we upgrade our computer?
- Why do I keep losing my keys?

...and on, and on, and on. PLEASE GIVE ME THE ANSWER!

The above questions are not unique to any specific program. They are common to all of us who genuinely want to see music programs thrive and prosper. They are also applicable to every band, orchestra, choir, etc., whether there are thirty or three hundred people involved.

Let us consider that the answer may not exist. Suppose quality music education is based on an infinite journey of questions? If so, then the process of learning becomes the focal point instead of some elusive destination. The ongoing questions serve as stepping stones to more intriguing concerns. Isn't there always room for improvement? (Yet another question!)

Such an assumed premise would lead us to see the joy of teaching lies in this endless expedition. Therefore, instead of avoiding or sidestepping uncomfortable or difficult questions, we should be embracing them, for they offer the fuel for positive forward momentum. A quick-fix answer might well void any further exploration and stop short of an incredibly beneficial idea.

For example, let us suppose a director is concerned about concert attendance. The question is, Why don't more people come to our concerts? If we shut down all thought provocation with a fast answer (i.e., "These people around here don't care about good music. All they think about is sports and cars."), we have eliminated any chance of creative experimentation and problem solving. We do have an answer, but also we still have the problem, which would suggest we went in a circle of self-deception.

Unfortunately, many (who are seeking the answer in the first place) will accept this answer as a given truth, thus stopping any further inquiry into the vital question. We still have no audience, but at least we have an answer as to why the predicament exists. Case closed.

Countless concerts will be performed to a small number of listeners year after year until finally someone becomes dissatisfied and reopens the question. At this point, the astute teacher will not accept the assumed answer, but will seek ways to put bodies in the concert hall. Of course, when that mission is accomplished, it will simply raise more questions: Where can we find a bigger auditorium? Can we do two performances? Should we have a matinee concert and an evening concert? Could we sell tickets to the event? A straightforward "No" to this second set of questions curbs any further discussion, whereas the pursuit of the answer not only moves us in a healthy direction, but also (you guessed it) generates more questions. And now we must deal with how to pay the rent on the larger facility, where to find two sets of ushers, what is a fair price for the tickets, and so forth.

There is nothing particularly revolutionary about this concept, but it tends to run opposite the popular theme of today's world. We are inundated with instant answers for life's questions and problems. We are trained to look for the quickest way to completion. Never mind if we fall short of the intended goal—if so, simply restate the goal and claim victory for a job well done. Such thinking will close off any questioning, introspective evaluation, or critical analysis, while in its place we have put the answer. It is analogous to putting a Band-Aid on a broken bone; we're only pretending to have solved the problem and it is certain to reappear, not to mention the pain caused along the way.

At this point, it would be an easy answer to view all of this as a pointless paradox, causing us to return to square one. However, when observing successful people who are daily addressing the very same questions, it is apparent they replace frustration and confusion with persistent examination, supported by their ongoing enthusiasm for improvement in every area of their program. They are not looking for the answer, but invite a dialog of questions, being wisely cautious of those all-too-easy pat answers. They have learned to enjoy the endless search and are well aware excellence is not a point of arrival, but rather the byproduct of the pilgrimage.

"Knowledge comes, but wisdom lingers. It may be difficult to store up in the mind a vast quantity of facts within a comparatively short time, but the ability to form judgments requires the severe discipline of hard work and the tempering heat of experience and maturity."
—Calvin Coolidge

The Best Advice Is: Don't Take Anyone's Advice...Find Out for Yourself

There is more to the title of this chapter than meets the eye. We all get advice, whether we want it or not. Likewise we give advice, whether people want it or not. Everyone is sharing information, offering thoughts about what to do, and certainly what *not* to do. A good friend once told me, "Advice is worth about what it costs. Nothing!" (I thought that was good advice.)

Advice never really rings true until a set of circumstances occurs which proves the reality of the advice: i.e., "Don't put your hand in the fire, it will burn." (Oh, sure. Then we put our hand in the fire and guess what? It burns.) Immediately we are painfully reminded of the advice we should have heeded. However, we are often given bogus advice. "Run, run, the sky is falling." We immediately cover our head with our burnt hand only to quickly realize we have been fooled and are now the brunt of the joke. Burnt or brunt, neither option is very desirable.

For most of us, advice needs to stand the test of time. If it continues to be accurate time and time again, we begin to rely on it, use it in our favor, and even share it with our family and friends. Solid advice will offer benefits which bring better conditions to life and can help us make decisions for our future.

The best advice I ever received came from my grandfather. Grandfathers usually give very good advice, because they have tried it out for several decades. Their counsel comes from years of research and development, and if they don't know by now, who does? Among the many pearls of wisdom Grandpa passed my way, this one ranked right at the top of his "Clues for a Better Life" list: *We become like the people we are around.*

He was adamant about this and constantly would point out different people's behavior to confirm his theory. He never believed that water seeks its own level, but rather that we could determine our level of proficiency by choosing our environment and our associates. His many lectures, though gentle in nature, were frequent reminders of how important it was to carefully choose "the best people possible" to be around. That advice served as the key factor in many of my decisions. It was, and still is, good, solid advice.

There are so many occasions when a conscious choice of what we are going to do can positively impact our future and the welfare of our students, and much of this depends on the people we are around, not to mention the people we *bring* around.

For example, if you had an unlimited budget, wouldn't you invite the finest clinician-teachers in the world to work with your students? Of course you would. You would also create a musical environment which would expose them to quality performers displaying exemplary musical habits and disciplines. You might add to your agenda a concert series featuring an array of superb performances, and quality would become the trademark of everyone your students met.

That would be a dream come true, but few people have access to that kind of extra revenue, so a more realistic option is to explore the use of audio and video tapes featuring the experts; or when any of influential personalities get within driving distance, you put the students in a van or bus and the mountain is taken to Mohammed. We know the harvest of such ventures will be bountiful and positive. It rarely (if ever) fails. Grandfather was right!

We all have had the experience of working with an extraordinary teacher, and when we are in the presence of such a person we reach beyond our known limits and discover we can perform at a higher level. In truth, the newfound talents and abilities were always within us, but the master teacher triggered something which catapulted us (the student/learner) to the next level. The mentor not only served as a role model, but also imparted valuable knowledge which helped unlock more of our human potential.

The obvious question is, *could* we have done it on our own? The answer is yes, but we must then ask, *would* we have done it on our own? According to Grandpa's advice, the due credit must be assigned to *the personal teacher we were around.*

One of the greatest contributions we can offer our students is to expose them to excellence in every facet of our music world. Play the best recordings of the finest literature, train their ears to recognize magnificent tone, blend, phrase, cadence, and dynamics. Search every catalog you can get your hands on and look for the latest video series by the leading authorities, and then make it a homework assignment to view them, study them, and learn from "the best of the best." Invite credible clinicians to come and spend time with your students so they can witness firsthand the value of personal commitment and self-discipline. Take them to hear good music in a concert hall. (It is not the same as when it is played through the speaker system in the rehearsal room or through a set of headphones. Give them the authentic experience, the real thing!) And, above all, when your students have the chance to be in an environment where there are a multitude of fantastic teachers who represent today's most respected professionals, do everything within your power to get them involved so *they will start to become like the people they are around.*

In a world where everyone you meet has a piece of advice, it is always exciting to discover bona fide wisdom which will never let you down. The fire *will* burn, the sky *is not* falling, and we do become like the people we are around.

Be around the best!

"The credit belongs to the man who is actually in the arena; whose face is marred by dust and sweat and blood; who strives valiantly; who errs and comes up short again and again; who knows the great enthusiasms, the great devotions, and spends himself in a worthy cause; who at the best knows in the end the triumph of high achievement; and who at the worst, if he fails, at least fails while daring greatly...."
—Theodore Roosevelt

The Solution to Success Is in the Mirror

"Our music program is terrible. The kids don't care, the parents don't care, the administration doesn't care, the community doesn't care; what am I supposed to do?! I have tried everything. They simply aren't motivated and we will never have a successful music program in this school...NEVER!"

The desperation of this music educator's situation is frightening. What chance do you think the students have with a teacher who is living with such a defeatist attitude? Is there any solution, or is it time to simply pull the plug and bring a merciful halt to the misery everyone is suffering?

In this situation it appears everyone is to blame (the students, parents, administrators and members of the community) for the bleak circumstances, and if that is so, it is time for some positive influence from an enthusiastic leader who refuses to accept the conditions as they are, but is committed to infusing life into the program and offering hope to everyone who eagerly seeks a pathway to success. Who could that savior be? Who is willing to go that extra mile? Who has the wherewithal to bring music back to the forefront of everyone's life?

The answer is quite simple: *it is the person we see when we look in the mirror.* There is the solution to the problem! The question is, Are we willing to pay the price? It means breaking old habits and developing new patterns that will allow us to generate the effect, rather than be "at the effect." We will have to take the road less traveled, and the journey can be very long and very lonely, but it leads to success— success for everyone who wants to be a part of excellence.

Unfortunately, we have become *masters of blame.* Every time something does not meet our expectations, we tend to blame someone or something. However, whenever we blame, we give up our power over the situation. We have, in fact, given into the circumstances and have allowed the situation to determine our reaction instead of our pro-action to determine the situation. This certain pathway to failure is so subtle, most of us don't realize we are on it. What's more, we will defend why we had to blame someone or something, which is just another coating of blame! How paradoxical!

There is a wonderful (and truthful) bit of wisdom that says: *Whether we think we can or whether we think we can't, we are always right.* If we as educators are convinced that "it won't work," then our minds lead us in the direction of the most dominant thoughts and we begin to focus on the evidence that proves our theory. In this case, we confirm our worst fears and confirm "it won't work."

The powerful human mind will always be right, therefore whatever we see as true, in effect becomes true. (Self-fulfilling prophecy.) The only way out of this downward spiral is to change (re-program) our mind to believe, "It can work." At the very moment of the acceptance of the new belief, we begin to refocus on the various aspects of the situation that proves us right, but this time we are right about the belief that things will be taking a turn for the better, and once again we are confirmed, "It will work."

Too simplistic, you say. (That's just more "being right" about the fact that it won't work and everything continues in the predictable old negative pattern. The mind wins, you lose. It's frustrating, isn't it? Which is exactly what got us in this predicament in the first place.) If we want to shift this and upgrade to a new level of living, we must leave the comfort zone and risk some new thoughts, new ideas, and even new experiences with an entirely new attitude.

Leaving our comfort zone is frightening. This fear will often serve as a barrier to keep us from taking that all-important step to a new understanding. We become sarcastic, cynical, and even hostile about those who challenge us to break away from those comfortable habits. It's not that we are satisfied, but rather afraid of what might be awaiting us in the unknown parts of life. As one person told me, "No, I don't want to change. I'm not really satisfied with my life, but if I gamble and make these personal changes, things might get worse than they already are, so it is just easier to stay where I am. At least I know how to handle life at this level." Is that living or just maintenance? Is that a positive role model for our students' attitudes?

On the other hand, there are many people who are exploring life at its fullest. They have learned to use fear as their ally and turn the energy of fear (which often holds us back) into the energy of risk and continue to add to their library of experiences by learning, growing, discovering, and enjoying the full range of dynamics in living.

Which person would you predict would be the most effective music educator? Which would inspire the students to jump headfirst into the artistry of music and learn a new language of self-expression? Which one would you like to be around if you were a student?

Which of these people do you see when you look in the mirror?

It is often uncomfortable to discuss being uncomfortable. These kinds of articles are not popular, for they challenge each of us (including the author) to come out of ourselves and reveal our insecurities. We are vulnerable and often defenseless, so the constant temptation is to run back inside our safe character and avoid any chance of the embarrassment of failure. (How ironic that this process assures failure and even is failure.) The only real security is to admit we are insecure, just as the only real competence is to admit we are incompetent. When we are willing to bring this truth forward and embrace it, we begin to empower ourselves and do not have to resort to blame, but can use that energy to start to take action to improve the conditions. What lies behind us and what lies ahead of us is pale compared to what lies within us. The answer is in the mirror!

The many cultures of the world have brought forth some remarkable wisdom. The following story, an ancient Hindu legend, is one that provokes a great deal of thought in a gently humorous way. Please understand it is not a religious message or an implication of suggested metaphysical beliefs, but rather a chance to understand the tremendous potential we all have.

At one time, all men on earth were gods. But they so sinned and abused the Divine, that Brahma, the god of all gods, decided that the power of the godhead should be taken away from man and hidden someplace where man would never find it and abuse it again.

"We will bury it deep in the earth," said the other gods.

"No," said Brahma, "because man will dig down in the earth and find it."

"Then we will sink it into the deepest ocean," they said.

"No," said Brahma, "because man will learn to dive and find it there too."

"We will hide it on the highest mountain," they said.

"No," said Brahma, "because man will some day climb every mountain on the earth and again capture the godhead."

"Then where can we hide it where man cannot find it?" asked the lesser gods.

"I will tell you," said Brahma, "hide it down in man himself. He will never think to look there."

Ah yes. We are once again reminded through this fable, *the solution to success is in the mirror.*

"For one human being to love another: that is perhaps the most difficult of all our tasks, the ultimate, the last test and proof, the work for which all other work is but preparation."
—*Rainer Maria Rilke*

The Importance of Role Models: My Starting Five

W hy would a person choose to dedicate his or her life to the field of music education? What set of circumstances guides an individual to commit to a journey unlike any other discipline in the school curriculum? When does one come to grips with the realization "teaching music is a joy beyond words?"

Many of us are music teachers because of our own music teachers. Role models have positively influenced all of us, and we may not realize their importance until several decades after the seed of teaching has been planted. There is certainly an unspoken bonding we all have with select educators in our lives, and for most of us, our music teachers/directors/educators are responsible for our lifelong involvement with music.

The following is a short tribute to the key people (my starting five) who made such a positive impact on my life.

THANKS, MOTHER. As a young boy, I can remember our home was filled with music, compliments of a console

Emerson hi-fi (pre-stereo!) which faithfully generated the talents of Count Basie, Oscar Peterson, the Teddy Wilson trio, and other select jazz artists. Though the record collection was not large, it was healthy.

The constant (and perhaps subliminal) musical message was a theme of our family. Neither Mom nor Dad are trained musicians, but they both possess an innate love of quality music and always made sure my ears were being exposed to the "right stuff." Piano lessons were as much a part of life as going to school; in fact, piano was required study before the much-favored drum set could be approached. My mother can sit down at the piano and play any song in any key. In spite of her inability to read music, she is a consummate musician. As my first real music educator, she taught me more about phrasing and cadence than anyone. How well I remember hearing a song on the radio and then asking Mom to be my accompanist for a living room performance of my own vocal rendition. She always knew which key would best suit my limited range, and would softly sing background harmony as I enjoyed center stage. When the melody line faltered, Mom was always there with a reinforcement of the melody and a strict reminder to listen carefully to the pitch. Little did I know what a priceless lesson in ear training was taking place.

With her tap-dancing studio connected to the house, every afternoon was spent doing homework with a background of feet in rhythm. How quickly I learned the necessity of subdivision and the crucial importance of "good time." To this day, my internal metronome automatically listens for the groove which gives motion to music. Mother's coaching is responsible for this as her words of the past still echo in my ears, "Don't force the beat. Let it get inside you."

THANKS, MISS SELLERS. Our small country school was

not particularly noted for anything with the exception of a rather unique vocal music teacher, Miss Dortha Sellers. From the first grade through graduation, she became a key person in the educational process. She was strict, committed, demanding, wonderfully sensitive, and unwilling to admit we were country folks incapable of performing quality music. Without question, Miss Sellers "made the difference" for me.

We not only had a huge choir, we were also saturated with all forms of vocal music: madrigals, barbershop, solos, swing choir (before there was such a thing), and a performance schedule which would challenge any professional touring group. She insisted on excellence in every aspect of our participation, and she got it. Although music was not a requirement, over 90% of the school body would spend fourth period crammed into an unacceptable rehearsal room learning the likes of Handel, Bach, and other masters. We did make a joyful sound and brought a new level of music to our community. How did she do it? Quite simply, she was a magnificent teacher.

THANKS, MR. McHENRY. Though instrumental music was not a priority for most students in the school, the last two years of high school band opened some new doors of opportunity, thanks to a remarkable new teacher who took a dismal group of instrumentalists and created a band, a real band! The talent level was minimal, at best, but that did not hinder Mr. McHenry from making believers out of all of us. Even Mother commented about how good the band sounded. I now understand what pain she suffered during some of those lean years when the ensemble desperately struggled to find the end of a composition. (Perfect pitch isn't always the perfect thing to have!) He was a model of persistence and personal tenacity. How well I remember telling him of my secret desire to be a band director and his quick, encouraging, and candid response, "If that is your dream, we better get started right now. There is no time to lose."

He was well aware of my lack of musical preparation and the competitive road ahead for anyone aspiring to go into the study of music; however, he never indicated this truth, but simply embraced the dream with me. During the last year of high school, every study hall was spent in the band room with Mr. McHenry helping with the beginners, learning the basics of every instrument, and sharing his wisdom while committing his advice to memory. Had it not been for this superb teacher, the first semester of college theory would have been the decisive blow of failure.

THANKS, MR. DUNN. College was not what I expected. As stated by one of my professors, "You're in over head. You are too far behind your classmates to catch up. Why don't you select another area of study?" This statement was confirmed by the fact that I was an alternate in the marching band. (Do you know how embarrassing that can be?) Once again, the muses extended their favor and brought another angel of mercy into my life, Mr. F. Earl Dunn, my college band director and a mentor beyond compare. While many discouraged the long uphill battle ahead, he took the opposite point of view and became a faithful confidant and to this day remains the number one counselor when seeking advice.

Mr. Dunn not only was a role model for quality music, he was also a master of organization, a disciplinarian to the point of perfectionism, thorough in every aspect of his professional career, and a teacher of teachers at the highest level. Unforgiving in his expectations, he intuitively knew which students would and wouldn't make it and stood by those of us who were willing to pay the price. There were never any special favors, no shortcuts for his favorites, no partiality ever shown, but rather a silent bond of allegiance read between the lines of his commanding style. He abhorred any kind of slipshod effort and never allowed a halfhearted attempt at any aspect of life. Favors were nonexistent and each day was a new opportunity to prove oneself. Past accomplishments carried no weight with Mr. Dunn. One's worth was based on the present moment contribution. A new meaning of personal integrity was extended via this select and loved educator.

THANKS, MR. METZENGER. Can you imagine what it was like when I walked into the office of Ed Metzenger, lauded timpanist with the Chicago Symphony Orchestra for thirty-four years? After stumbling through a rather simple piece of music, this gruff-looking old man put his arm around me and said, "Son, we have much work to do. Are you sure you want to be a band director?" With tears in my eyes and a lump in my throat, I responded affirmatively and pleaded with him to accept me as his student. From that day forth, I was in the presence of a musical wizard and a gentle bear with an unlimited supply of compassion. Every lesson was a textbook experience in patience.

While many stood in line to "learn from the master," he always, always, made time for me. Extra lessons "with Metz" were commonplace. Studio chats of hidden advice were encouraged, and we all proudly boasted of being "one of Metz's boys." Though his sense of educational responsibility did not match that of others at the university, he offered a pragmatic viewpoint of music and created an equality which opened communication at a level of personal inquisition I had never experienced before, or since. Secure in his own talents (and being) Metz displayed a love and understanding for the art which was poetic. He *was* the music. Though he never attended college, his knowledge of music was overwhelming. He had performed with the greatest of the greats. Gershwin was his personal friend, vaudeville was his training ground, and these two extremes (and everything between) made him a walking encyclopedia of unwritten musical secrets of success. Like eager first graders, we would sit around listening to his tales of world premières, playing for the most renowned conductors of all time, and talking to "the ladies" when he was the pit drummer in the Chicago burlesque theaters. Metz offered a classic and necessary methods class in life. He did it unknowingly and with a sense of genuineness not found in any educational psychology textbook.

His ultimate gift came in the summer of 1972 when he agreed to come out of retirement and serve as my applied teacher while working on my doctorate. At the time he was not in the best of health. When I arrived for the graduate school session, I called him to say hello and arrange a time to get together. The next day I was called into the music office for a personal meeting with the Director of the School of Music who informed me that Metz had phoned and was willing to serve as my private teacher if I so wished. His love of music knew no end; his legend lives on through his students. How lucky I am to be one of "Metz's boys."

THANK YOU, Mother, Miss Sellers, Mr. McHenry, Mr. Dunn, and Mr. Metzenger. You represent my answers to the questions asked in the opening of this article. You made the difference for me. You were (and still are) the foundation and role models for a life worth living. May I be the steward of your most important gift and pass it on through teaching to an exciting generation of musicians yet to come.

This article first appeared in slightly different form in the book *Life in the Music Classroom.*
Copyright © 1992 by Music Educators National Conference.
Used by permission of MENC.

"It is just the little difference between the good and the best that makes the difference between the artist and the artisan. It is just the little touches after the average man would quit that make the master's fame."
—Orison Swett Marden

The State of Your Art

The state of the art is, by definition, *the level of development (procedure, process, technique, or science) reached at any particular time as a result of modern technology.* It is the cutting edge, the latest and most effective product or data available, and as we all know, it is never static, but constantly being pushed forward, fueled by the human desire for excellence.

What is the state of *your* art?

Before anyone can answer this, we must first identify which part of your agenda is in question. Most people would immediately think the word *art* would imply conducting, individual instrumental technique, interpretation, score study, etc. However, let's extend the boundaries of possibilities to include the rehearsal environment and take a critical view of an often-overlooked area that plays a crucial role in the effectiveness of your ensemble's performance: the area of organization and management. We must all admit that herein lies much room for growth and improvement.

Have you ever been listening to a wonderful performance and suddenly there is a blatant wrong note that immediately draws your attention and then you think, "Ouch...too bad...I'll bet that gets cleaned up real fast in the next rehearsal." However, if it is a weak overall performance, the individual infractions are almost ignored and your mental conversation shifts to, "Oh my gosh, there is a ton of work to do with this group. Someone really needs to get in there and do some fundamental teaching. It will be a long time before there will ever be any artistic performance from this ensemble."

The performers probably feel much the same, except their inner voices might say, "Why should I even try? We are so pathetic. What good will it do to practice? There are so many bad sounds it would cover up any good ones that I might contribute! Nobody in the group cares anyway!"

This negative logic is easy to understand, particularly when described in musical terms. We all understand the harmonic components necessary to establish a state-of-the-art musical performance. However, can we draw a similar parallel to the rehearsal environment? Though this may be uncomfortable, it is the key to success for those educators who understand the importance of students' developing quality habits in every aspect of their lives.

If you walked into a rehearsal facility and observed instrument cases strewn about, percussion equipment left out and being used as make-shift tables, wastepaper baskets running over with paper and empty soda cans, coats thrown here and there, music lying on the floor, chairs and stands scattered from wall to wall, what would you think? Can you see that this might have some detrimental effect on the musical aspect of the program? If there is this kind of lack of concern for the physical atmosphere, is there a chance it would bleed over into the rehearsal habits?

To answer these questions, let's simply reverse the scenario. Enter the same rehearsal hall where the room is neatly set up, the instruments are carefully stacked or in lockers, the floors are free from debris—all this dictating a level of discipline that could be transferred directly to the musical expectations. Would it have an impact on the rehearsal habits? One can quickly see the ramifications of one domain (environment) will certainly influence the outcome of another area (the musical product).

What is the state of your art in respect to your environment? Would it be worth devoting some time and energy in the development of this phase of your program? We are in such an urgent rush to spend time on the technical aspect of the music, we might well be overlooking one of the subliminal handicaps preventing us from attaining that much-desired goal. Without knowing it, we could be sabotaging the forward progress of the group by ignoring the environmental messages the students are receiving about acceptable standards.

Certainly this is not to suggest that a few hours spent straightening up the rehearsal facilities will make the clarinets play in tune. However, it may make the individual musicians "strive to play in tune" with a bit more artistic attitude based on their assessed conclusion that you are serious about seeking quality in every facet of their musical experience, including their surroundings.

The next step is to make your state of the art become their state of the art. Once the standards are set, they must be owned, administered, and carried out by the members of the group. Just as a fine performer is responsible for intonation, balance, blend, command of the musical part, etc., the members of the organization need to be responsible for the environment. This requires the same amount of individual consideration and attention they give to playing a phrase, caring for a reed, and proper posture.

If we expect a group to perform artistically "on stage," we

should expect no less from them "off stage," and that performance should not just be limited to the time from the downbeat to the release; it is an ongoing effort of self-improvement for the students and certainly for us, their teachers and role models.

For most of us, it is much easier to ignore a disorganized music library than it is to sidestep bad intonation. After all, the music library is not going to be seen by the public at the next concert, but the audience will certainly be listening to the band's performance. We are tempted to just close our office door to avoid personal embarrassment during the booster meeting rather than simply sit down and organize all of the things stacked on and beside the desk. It's not that we don't know what to do, it's just another task that easily drops to the bottom of the "to do" list. We become our own worst enemy and seem to forget the contagious habits of our daily patterns will appear (good or bad) in the ensemble's achievement, *the state of their art.*

We may be encouraged when we remember the importance of our work. We do what we do to make life better for those who are sharing our journey. This gives more credence to the need to extend the state of our art. In the words of Bryan Lindsay,

> *Let the arts inform you and guide you toward excellence. Keep the arts at the center of your consciousness, because beyond all else, the arts will best inform you of the nature of human quality.*

We have the wherewithal to empower the students to live a better life. Rarely will any group exceed the expectations of the director. Just as the train follows obediently behind the engine, the young musicians will quickly adapt to the demands and commands of the maestro. With that truth in mind, it is of great importance that we constantly remind ourselves of the importance of our total educational presentation both on and off the podium by asking, What is the state of my art?

"I am only one,
But still I am one,
I cannot do everything,
But still I can do something...."
—Edward Everett Hale

Waving the Flag for Music: A Useful Tool for Advocacy

For those of us who are deeply involved in teaching music, it is apparent what an important role the arts, specifically music, play in the development of any student. It is unthinkable to consider preparing a child for life without a solid background in music, but it is obvious we need to remind others of this reality. The following is a collage of "reasons why" it is important for music to be a fundamental part of every child's learning, and this essay can be used in its entirety or excerpted as needed when addressing any group who needs to be informed. Just as there can be no music without learning, no education is complete without music.

If we believe schools exist to develop a child for a productive and meaningful life, then we must look at the contribution music makes in scope of the curriculum. The rationale below is broken into four main areas of focus: intrinsic value of music, academic and peer associations, preparation for life, and building individual positive self-worth. Each of the four main reasons stands on its own, but together they present a powerful combination.

INTRINSIC VALUE

The process of making music is the reward. Unlike many things we do in school, music is music for its own sake. Music is beauty within itself. It offers a microcosm of life, for the essence of life is in the living: the journey, not the destination; the process, not the product; and ultimately the purpose, not the outcome—much like the man who fishes not to catch fish, but for the pleasure of fishing, and who throws caught fish back in the water so he can fish some more.

Music offers an opportunity to experience the pleasure of self-expression at a new level, opening exciting vistas of self-satisfaction. So much of our educational system is "impressionistic." Student are given the material and the better they can repeat it, the higher the grade they get. There is little chance to "create" or add a personal touch to the assignments. In fact, individuality is often discouraged.

Music class is a place which is "expressionistic" and students are encouraged to put their own thoughts and feelings into their music making. This offers a much-welcomed change from the normal learning process.

The veteran musician knows that music speaks to something more subtle than the intellect; it speaks to the very soul of human kind. Music is woven into the fiber of our life, our spirit. We are moved, changed, alerted to a new sense of knowing by experiencing music. Think of your reaction when you hear Handel's *Messiah*, or witness a fine band marching down the street at the local parade or feel the heart-wrenching plea of a talented blues singer. We know there is happy music, sad music, music for celebrations, and music to soothe wounded emotions. What else can generate such feelings?

Music stretches one's understanding of self, which in turn helps us understand others. And every musician will quickly tell you it stimulates a part of the mind which opens our imagination, bringing about a highly intellectual activity we have come to call *joy*.

ACADEMIC AND PEER ASSOCIATION

We become like the people with whom we associate. The world of behavioral psychology continues to point out the reality of personality modification through peer association. We are adaptable creatures and we quickly conform to our environment (whatever it may be) to perpetuate our survival. Therefore, if our children are going to become academically strong, it would reason they should be spending time in the presence of other successful students. With this in mind, consider these findings: Students in music are scoring 20 to 40 points higher on SAT tests, and the longer a student participates in the school music program, the higher the SAT scores.

Music develops the appetite for learning and creates habits of self-discipline and personal tenacity which carry over into every facet of school. Young musicians are skilled at concentration, alertness, memory, and self-control. These attributes are basic for success in higher education, but more importantly, in succeeding at life.

There is a strong correlation between music and the disciplines of science and math—music uses the same reasoning processes. And the social requirements of group effort and communication, along with the development of motor skills, are an integral part of every music lesson.

Many have said that their musical background helped to develop the "forgotten side of the brain," for music encourages us to use acquired knowledge to deal with various aspects of life: values, ethics, creative decision making, and problem solving. Music is not an answer, but a set of questions requiring the individual to "discover the answer." Life is not about answers, but rather a quest to find the answers, and the more profound the question, the more exciting the search for the answer.

PREPARATION FOR LIFE

We all want our children to experience a healthy, happy, and prosperous life and to enjoy themselves in the process. There are certainly mental tools which aid in this goal, and music is crucial in honing those tools:

CREATIVITY. Music opens new horizons of the mind and supports wonderment, imagination, appreciation, and sensitivity. Creativity is the source of possibility and is a mental muscle that must be trained and exercised often.

COMMUNICATION. Music is a language beyond words. Music can only be explained with music because of its various styles, textures, tempos, and dynamics. It can elicit an emotion. Think of what television or movies would be without music warning us of the impending danger, or setting the mood for the festivities of a wedding. Music truly stirs the soul of man. No words or visual display can come close to the emotional impact of music.

CRITICAL ASSESSMENT. Music is one of the key areas where an individual can develop a consistency between intellectual and emotional understanding. Here is the chance to bridge the cognitive and affective data of life, which many feel is the recipe of genius. Music offers one the chance to conceptualize, not just respond. In other words, we can create formulas instead of just solutions, and we can be proactive rather than re-active. We can open the mind and avoid tunnel vision—and in doing so, come up with discerning opinions which develop quality character.

COMMITMENT. It is almost impossible to be "partially committed" to music. One may quit on a test, refuse to turn in an assignment, or just not be aware of what is going on in a lecture class, but the participation level in music requires a focus of attention unlike most subjects in school. Music causes one to learn persistence and the value of "not giving up," even when there is the temptation to throw in the towel. Many have pointed to "stay power" as one of the greatest personal attributes in our society. Welcome to one of the key benefits of the study of music.

BUILDING INDIVIDUAL POSITIVE SELF-WORTH

Every individual is a unique and important source of human potential. To be able to offer our personal artistic signature to any endeavor offers us a special place in life. Music does give us a vehicle to critically express our individuality while supporting our fellow beings.

In a very important way, it allows us to know who we are and answer the question we all face, "Why do I exist?" In music, we do matter, we do make a difference, we do have value. Nobody can make the same contribution to the art as we alone can.

Music offers us a balance between what we take and what we give, and through giving (or expressing), our self-image rises because we have brought something unique to the world. We are unique, exclusive, and important. We have value as a vital member of society, and the awareness of this reality encourages us to be responsible in our actions as a contributing member of the community.

In today's world, so many young people seem to be lost, swimming about in a maze of quick fixes, desperately looking for something other than fashion labels with which to identify. If their musical talents are developed, nurtured, and sought, then their value increases, and they have worth...self-worth, the most important component of a fruitful life.

This chapter certainly does not suggest the study of music to the exclusion or expense of other subject areas, but merely states the fundamental importance of the music in the basic development of the student. It is the birthright of every child, and it becomes our duty to see it is delivered.

There is an important duty we all share as music educators, and it has been dormant in many job outlines. Although we can turn our backs on the plight of music education, it is our moral duty to wave our own flag. Although we may feel incompetent as lobbyists for our own cause, the alternative is extinction.

The questions are bold and simple:

If not now, when?
If not here, where?
If not you, who?

Just as there can be no music without learning, there can be no education without music. Let the music begin.

"There is no higher religion than human service. To work for the common good is the greatest creed."
—Albert Schweitzer

The Future of Music Education: The Harmony Begins at Home

We are certainly living through an uncertain era in the evolution of music education. In the midst of financial cutbacks, curricular reform, and new accountability standards, the validity of the arts as a part of the academic schedule is constantly being challenged.

National and regional organizations are mounting campaigns to defend music in our schools and educate politicians, lawmakers, and every administrative body about the importance of this fundamental study. Already we have seen entire music programs being cut by the stroke of a pen or relegated to a token offering during the activity period. For those of us who believe deeply in the value of music, music education, and all the arts, these cuts are an appalling discriminatory violation of every child's birthright.

Thoughts and questions naturally come to every dedicated music teacher:

What can I do to help? Is this hopeless? I have no power. Nobody listens to me. This is somebody else's job. They'll probably take care of it without my input. I'm a teacher, not a lobbyist. You don't expect me to deal with curriculum issues, do you? How could I possibly have an impact of any worth? This is too confusing and really doesn't effect my students...and on, and on, and on.

There may not be a quick solution, but there is certainly something we all can do, and it doesn't involve any major change in how we teach, in who we are, or in the focus of our daily patterns. We don't have to march down the main street of town waving flags or lock ourselves in the instrument room to dramatically draw the media's attention. Although we certainly need to be vocal about our belief in the basic value of music and other arts, we must first do this by example within our own profession.

We speak of harmony, blend, and balance, but do we exercise these important cooperative qualities outside the rehearsal? As music educators, do we project a professional attitude of mutual support, common consensus, and shared values? Do we validate our fellow teacher? In essence, do we portray a community working in harmony and dedicated to the proliferation of a balanced platform of agreed standards?

In a recent discussion with a high-ranking administrator (one who had the power to determine the future of the music program in the entire school system), he offered some uncomfortable, but thought-provoking, opinions based on his perception of the music staff.

He brought these frustrating thoughts to the conversation: "I do not disagree that music is an important part of the child's learning. That's not the issue. You must understand that we administrators are charged with the responsibility of fulfilling the mandates set forth by our State Board of Education. There are a given number of minutes in the school day and the basic academic requirements for each student must be accounted for in the planning. Our task is to put this together to abide by the law while still maintaining the educational values of our local community. Music is viewed as an important part of our curriculum by everyone, including me. Every department is aggressively seeking their fair share of the school day, and I design the schedule based on the recommendations of the curriculum committee. We certainly do not want to threaten or damage our music program; we feel it is vitally important. But to be perfectly honest, it is difficult to get the members of the music faculty to agree on what they want! Short of building the entire academic offering around music, we cannot seem to come to any kind of consensus with these people. I take offense when someone says I'm opposed to music or the arts. That is not true, but we are often deadlocked by the members of the music faculty. How can we reach agreement with them when they can't reach agreement with one another? The most convenient way for me to solve this problem is to simply restrict music offerings, cut back the number of music specialists, and move ahead."

Needless to say, there was a lapse in the conversation. The introspective thoughts that followed were unpleasant, confrontational, and difficult to face. My friend was not being hostile, reactionary, or even condescending. He was perplexed, frustrated, distraught, and very bewildered. He wanted to help, but kept running into obstacles set up by the very people he was committed to serving.

These grave questions then went through my mind: *Are we guilty of sabotaging ourselves? In our effort to win the battle, are we losing the war? Do we see the global ramifications of our actions? Could we be our own worst enemy?*

Fortunately, in this case, the administrator did not choose the path of least resistance and was flexible enough to oblige many of the requests and demands of the music department. (He also had a background in music and two children who were part of the music program. Can we always count on this kind of inside-trader help?)

Educational reform is a way of life. This is not an issue that will pass by and everyone will live happily ever after. All areas of study will continuously be challenged and reviewed. We, as music educators, will be required to come forward and offer our expertise, and to explain why music should be a part of the school day. In that moment in time, it would behoove us to be aligned with our fellow music compatriots.

Perhaps you are a "one-man show." Your department meetings may be held at the local restaurant as you make and second each motion. If that's the case, it then becomes a matter of blending your advocacy with that of your students, parents, administration, and community. However, if you share the joy of teaching music with others of the same discipline, take advantage of the power of cooperation. It certainly doesn't mean you have to agree on every aspect of every subject. If there is a difference of opinion on methodology, pedagogy, interpretation, or whatever, find a way to agree to disagree, but don't let it turn into animosity that will divide your common direction or put the "big picture" in jeopardy. Deal with differences behind closed doors and walk out united in the shared goal of music education for every child.

One phrase has been spoken by many and it seems we should all heed its haunting message: *We either hang together or we hang separately.* The reality dictates we need to combine our efforts and energies for the benefit of all students who want to learn more about the most exciting language common to all mankind: MUSIC.

Part Two

Achieving Excellence in Teaching Music

"The goal of education is to discipline yourself to achieve mastery."

Achieving Excellence in Teaching Music

We all have our examples of excellent teachers. For many of us, certainly those reading this book, one or more of our music teachers serve in that role. So many choose to be a part of this profession because of a former music teacher. Did you?

What determines *excellence* in music education? What is it that makes a particular teacher so effective? What common thread do those very special teachers have that sets them apart from all others in our school experiences? And how do we pass along this understanding to the new breed of educators who will determine the future of music education?

Countless doctoral dissertations have been devoted to the study of the characteristics of successful music educators. The personality traits are not necessarily the same; in fact, they are often quite different. Successful teacher "A" may be an authoritarian and in charge of every decision in the program. Successful teacher "B" might create a totally different atmosphere with a very democratic approach involving the students in all aspects of choice making. How can they come from such opposite ends of the spectrum and still attain a similar success pattern? Might I suggest the answer not be

measured by their *efficiency,* but rather their *effectiveness.*
Efficiency is doing things right.
Effectiveness is doing right things.

Excellence in music education is about doing right things: being *effective.* The teaching habits of great teachers are an amplification of the individual's personality. If the teacher is sincere, ethical, committed, knowledgeable, and vitally interested in helping the students achieve mastery, success is inevitable. The teacher's pathway in achieving excellence may not be as important as their personal conviction in reaching the goal. We seem to intuitively know who these inspired educators are and we are drawn to them. We understand they believe in our talents and capabilities and are dedicated to seeing us succeed. Simply put, *we trust them.*

This particular section of *The Joy of Inspired Teaching* spotlights some of the proven success patterns of master teachers. Enjoy learning from those who continue to bring new insights to music education in a way that inspires many of us to carry on their mission.

"One difference between savagery and civilization is a little courtesy. There's no telling what a lot of courtesy would do."
—Cullen Hightower

Creating a Positive Learning Atmosphere

As teachers we all have a desire to present valuable information to our students. We want them to understand the importance and the impact of our presentation. There is a desire to leave every class with a sense of personal accomplishment and the feeling that we presented the students with data that will better their lives.

Unfortunately, that isn't always the case, is it? As an educator, what is your greatest frustration? Is it the crowded schedule? The required curriculum? The lack of facilities? The inadequate equipment? The poor financial support? Although all of these issues may bring about some anxiety, it seems that most teachers are concerned about the students' comprehension of the material presented.

Did they "get it"?

Did they learn in a way they can integrate the subject matter into their daily patterns? Can they draw upon this knowledge to improve their art form? There is often a huge gap between the teacher's presentation and the students' perception of the material shared. How can we bridge that chasm and end the mutual student/teacher frustration?

Communication is not what we say, but rather what they get.

Simply standing in front of a class and offering information is not teaching. The teaching process only happens when there is an exchange. Much like our modern day computer modem, before there can be any transfer of material, both the transmitter and the receiver must be operative, using the same language, and programmed to accept this process. If either computer is not properly set up, it will be an unsuccessful venture. (Those of you who have explored the high-tech world are well aware of the frustration when the process does not work!) The teaching/learning endeavor is much the same: both parties must be in the right mode if there is going to be the needed delivery and reception of the lesson(s).

When the computer transaction fails, we review the instructions and try again. If we still are not getting results, we call someone who knows about computer modems. When all else fails, we dial that magic "tech support" number and have an expert talk us through the procedure. In other words, we don't give up until we have accomplished our goal. If nothing else, it is a good lesson in persistence and tenacity. The computer simply will not settle for less than "the right way," and it doesn't care if we are frustrated or not; the computer demands we be correct before it will accept our instructions. We can abuse it, confuse it, refuse it, (and even threaten to lose it!) but it stoically sits there on the desk and awaits the input of the proper commands. (Computers are the master teacher of patience.)

Students are far less resilient, far less demanding, and we are never quite sure if they really understand. It is much easier to "give up" on the student than it is on the computer. Even if they do not comprehend the material we present, we can always say they didn't fulfill their learning responsibility. Can you envision saying that to a computer? It's pointless, isn't it?

If positive learning is to occur, it requires a two-step process:

1. The student must be mentally programmed to be ready to accept the material.
2. The data must be worthwhile and have substantive value.

It seems so simple, doesn't it? Any credible teacher will make certain that the lesson plan is built upon solid information. The second step of the equation is a direct reflection of our own study, planning, and continued research. However, if we dwell only on this facet of the formula, we will be unsuccessful. If the student is not in the receive mode, the transmission of material will be futile.

With that in mind, let us look carefully at the problem that faces many of us: how do we get the students to want to learn? Noted educational psychologist Stephen Glenn says when students are in an environment where they are encouraged to risk (and often fail), they are much more eager to become involved in the learning process. Failure is not something to be concerned about, but becomes another stepping stone in the journey of goal attainment. However, if their failure results in reprimands, shame, guilt, pain, or blame, they quickly learn to take the path of least resistance and begin practicing self-defense rather than focusing their energies on learning. Once the walls of self-protection go up, there is little chance that new information can get to the student. You could well give the finest lesson in the history of humankind, but unless the student is ready, all is lost.

As teachers, when we address a student (or anyone), we must be certain we do not threaten their ego or violate their human dignity. This does not mean that we simply sit back and avoid any sense of discipline; quite the contrary. There can be no learning without discipline, but we must be wise in the way we create and sustain a healthy learning atmosphere.

When things are going awry, we often take the short cut by addressing the character of the student rather than the inappropriateness of the behavior. This appears to be a solid solution, for it usually gets the student (as well as the rest of the class) to focus, and the behavior problems seem to disappear, at least momentarily. However, the student goes through the mental processes of resentment, revenge, and retreat. In most cases, the third option, retreat, is the best choice. They sit in class, well-behaved, quietly going through the motions, and learning nothing.

If we substitute encouragement for criticism and praise, we then offer that same student the chance to fail, and immediately they try again, and again, and again, until they master the assigned material. They understand we are not going to judge their performance, but rather join them in the process of learning. The student, in turn, becomes encouraged (in the presence of courage) and their acceptance of our advice becomes much greater. They realize we are an ally in the process and not a threat to their ego or their dignity. We merely adjust their behavior so they can benefit from their efforts.

Part one of our successful teaching formula is now in place.

There is one major flaw in the analogy between a computer modem and student learning. We can become very frustrated with the computer and unload our wrath on its emotionless screen and storm out of the room in a fit of anxious frustration, but when we come back, the computer will forgive us and we can pick up right where we left off. That is not the case with students. They remember. They carry the scars of our outbursts with them for a lifetime. Their sense of trust is damaged. They hurt...and often want to hurt us back. The computer doesn't care, the human does, and that's what makes us human.

Do you know any computers that can sing or play an instrument without being humanly manipulated? I don't.

Perhaps the frustrations we experience as teachers *should* be the schedules, the curricula, the equipment, etc. It *should not* be the students, for they represent the ultimate in human potential. They are the thinkers, feelers, and doers. Unlike a computer, they do not have a set amount of memory. They are limitless.

Every day, we should be challenged to create an environment that is conducive to risk and failure so each student will be safe and secure in the learning process, rather than retreating to a comfort zone where survival becomes a higher priority than personal growth. *Let the music begin!*

"We cannot tell what may happen to us in the strange medley of life. But we can decide what happens in us; how we can take it, what we can do with it, and that is what really counts in the end. How to take the raw stuff of life and make it a thing of worth and beauty; that is the test of living."
—Joseph Fort Newton

The Secret Ingredient of Master Teachers: Enthusiasm!

In the field of education, we are constantly reminded of the value of a qualified mentor. This truth is proven by the fact that many of us have become teachers because of a teacher. Our chosen discipline or area of study is often heavily influenced by the desire to model a former educator—and this seems most prominent in the area of the arts, specifically music.

Whether it is the emotional involvement that comes with any musical performance, or the extended amount of time we spend with the music teacher, or even the personal relationships developed as a healthy byproduct of the extra rehearsals and family atmosphere of the music class (or maybe a combination of all of these reasons), we know there is more to music than "just another class in the school day."

Something very special happens in music rehearsals that seems to have more of an impact on students than any other facet of education.

Do you remember your special teacher? What was the characteristic about the individual that inspired you to devote your life to teaching music? If you could focus on one attribute, what would it be? These questions have been asked by many, and more often than not, the answer is: the teacher's enthusiasm for the subject. It's true, isn't it? Those extraordinary mentors were the ones who were always on fire, wonderfully passionate, predictably excited, and extremely enthusiastic about their life's purpose—teaching the love of music, and loving to teach it.

Most college curricula do not have a class entitled, Enthusiasm 101. Perhaps they should. Where does one learn this personality trait that is the key to effective education? Does it just happen one day? Do we keep learning and adding more data to our minds, and then, all of a sudden, enthusiasm appears and we become obsessed with sharing the information with others?

In truth, most of us learned to be enthusiastic by being in the presence of an enthusiastic person. We became caught up in the charismatic communication of the teacher on the podium or in the studio, and began to emulate this same ardor when we are given our first teaching responsibilities. It is at that point we discover the "joy of inspired teaching," and the importance of the mission. That process, in itself, will generate enthusiasm.

We have many competent teachers in the profession, but those who are most effective also possess that magical quality, enthusiasm. It's undefinable, predictably unpredictable, wildly contagious, and the fuel for exploring the uncharted territory of human potential; it helps to push the art form one more orbit above its present position, to reach further than we think the mind can stretch, and to discover musical expression at a new level. All of this comes from enthusiasm, and these heights are rarely achieved without it.

What is enthusiasm? *Webster's New Collegiate Dictionary* offers this definition: *The belief in special revelations of the Holy Spirit; something inspiring zeal forever.* And on that same page, Webster goes further to tell us about the enthusiast: *One who is ardently attached to a cause, or pursuit. The one who gives completely to whatever engages his or her interest.* The derivation of the word, *en + theos*, means: *Filled with the spirit in the presence of God.*

We quickly see the origin of the word has religious implications and, through time, has been transferred to modern language to mean a zealous person, one who is devoted to promoting "the spirit" of whatever the chosen cause. This is a perfect description of those select mentors who brought us to the forefront and peaked our curiosity by demonstrating the art of "giving themselves completely to the subject matter."

Unfortunately, enthusiasm is often misinterpreted as cheap theatrics, over-dramatization, or even a substitute for credible information. The vibrant educator who demonstrates this quality may be the target of ridicule. However, the master teacher who can deliver substantive material with a spirit of passion that opens the minds and ignites the imagination is the mentor who makes the difference. It is at this point that the student becomes his or her own teacher and a peak learning experience is brought to the classroom. Herein lies the "magic moment" when the individual makes choices that will dictate life patterns. All of this happens because of an enthusiastic teacher.

If it is such a positive attribute, why don't more teachers display their fervor?

To be enthusiastic means:
• standing apart from the masses
• putting forth extra personal energy
• being willing to deal with the skeptics and cynics

- avoiding the temptation to quit or give up
- always finding something worthwhile in every situation
- living life with a purpose
- constantly growing and learning
- embracing the bad with as much love and understanding as the good

That is quite an agenda to complete and one that takes a tremendous level of self-discipline; however, the benefits far exceed any measurable form of wealth. In essence, enthusiasm makes life worth living. The introspective question we must all ask ourselves is, can we afford *not* to be enthusiastic?

One of our great modern day philosophers and theologians, Norman Vincent Peale, offers these words about enthusiasm:

> "Think enthusiastically about everything. If you do, you will put a touch of glory in your life. If you love your work with enthusiasm, you'll shake it to pieces. You'll love it into greatness, you'll upgrade it, you will fill it with prestige and power."

Isn't that what we all want to do with our lives? The purpose of life is to live life for a purpose. We as music educators have the opportunity to generate enthusiasm countless times each and every day. Bemoaning the fact we have had ten percent cut from our budget, or the scheduled concert is in conflict with an athletic event, or the music store didn't deliver the repaired bass clarinet, or whatever, is certainly important to the success of the program, but it is inconsequential compared to the fundamental charge of our profession, our art, our reason to be: to uplift every child we touch to a new level of appreciation and understanding about music.

Now that is a challenge that deserves to be met with a positive enthusiasm.

It's time to enthusiastically strike up the band!

"It is one of the beautiful compensations of this life that no one can sincerely try to help another without helping himself."
—Charles Dudley Warner

The Wisdom of Enthusiasm or the Enthusiasm of Wisdom

Most of us approach each new school year with a very positive desire to make it the "best year of our career." The all-too-quick summer respite has once again helped us recharge mentally and emotionally. The new academic year is waiting, *ready or not!*

What will make this year's group special? What can we do as educators to insure a successful year for the students, the program, and ourselves? Is there something we can do to dictate a rewarding experience for everyone involved?

Quite simply, the answer is an unequivocal, yes. The blueprint for the upcoming semesters is a manifestation of what is in our mind. How would you describe your band or choir, your performances, the rehearsal discipline of the students, your communication with the administration, your rapport with colleagues, etc.? *We tend to become like our most dominant thoughts.* Knowing this, it would seem we should begin to envision an uplifting year of personal and professional growth and the attainment of excellence in every facet of the program.

Although the logic is simple, there will be many who will enthusiastically create their list of reasons their organization will *not* succeed. Those personal seeds of doubt will take root and produce a predictable harvest. Unfortunately, the students who participate in such a program will live through a year of gloom and doom. It hardly seems fair, does it? Particularly when music or dance is about creating beauty, enjoying harmony, and learning lifelong concepts such as cooperation, self-discipline, development of potential, commitment, dedication, and a host of other personal attributes.

Isn't it time we redirected our energies to exploring the unlimited potential which every student brings to the performance rather than establishing limits of artistic confinement? Before any organization can reach a new level of performance, it requires the person in charge (the director...*you*) to believe it can be accomplished and move in that given direction. Although this statement might seem a bit uncomfortable (particularly to someone who is *certain* the circumstances are controlling our future), it should be just the opposite—for it offers the opportunity to embrace a new level of possibilities and infuse the performing groups with a powerful forward momentum. The sky's the limit!

There is not a performance educator in this country who does not want the best for his or her group. However, it is often easy to get entangled in the day-to-day problems and begin to accept mediocrity. Soon we find ourselves defending the very standards we abhor. As our friend Calvin Coolidge said, *"Argue for your limitations and you get to own them."*

Calvin would have held a more favorable position in the history books had he heeded his own words, but his message cuts right to the essence of the issue: Let us not waste precious time explaining why something *cannot* work, but let us instead find alternatives as we journey to the creation of a quality performance program.

If we could somehow combine the wisdom of the veteran director with the enthusiasm and eagerness of the young teacher, we would be well on the road to success. This combination is unfailing, and a short review may offer some good food for thought as we begin the new year.

1. *The short cut doesn't exist.* There is no back door to musical success. Regardless of equipment, scheduling, budget, color of uniforms, or any other factor, the final performance will be a reflection of the hours spent in quality rehearsals combined with dedicated practice of the individual students. Certainly there are many outside factors which can embellish one's ability, but there is no substitute for good-old-fashioned woodshedding. Time on task is the most certain investment one can make. The payoff will always be there.

One of the most valuable concepts we teach through a performance group is the understanding of *process* over *product.* Much has been written about the world of instant gratification, and we know this has become an all-too-common theme in our society. Certainly there are many benefits to a microwave oven, but it can often lead to a misrepresentation of the meaning of quality living. As much as our American "the more the better" credo has infiltrated every part of education, the truth is the *journey,* not the *destination,* is what counts. In a rather paradoxical twist, the shortcut is really the long haul.

2. *Enthusiasm is the fuel for success.* Enthusiasm is often misread as a rather frivolous approach to teaching a serious discipline. However, when we begin to dissect the components of our most successful role models, we see they are filled with a *pathos* (passion) to teach young people about

the joy of discovering a new language, a new art, a way to combine and express logic and feeling through music. Our mission is to open a new realm of possibilities to the young creative mind and allow them the tools to discover their own worth and share it with others. What greater gift could we possibly bring to the growth of a child?

As a role model, what are we projecting to our students about our own love for the band, orchestra, choir, or drill team?

There may not be a great deal we can do about budget cutbacks or changing of the class schedule, but we *can* control the time we have with our students and pledge ourselves to give them the most substantive information available as they learn.

"The most essential factor is persistence, the determination never to allow your energy or enthusiasm to be dampened by the discouragement that must inevitably come."
—James Whitcomb Riley

Criticize in Private, Praise in Public

We all want attention. Psychologists tell us it is the number-one payoff for the human creature. Attention confirms our very existence. In many cases, it tells us we are needed. *The need to be needed* is one of the distinctions between man and other animals; in fact, for many it is more important than survival itself. Even those people who say they don't really want attention often say so because it gets them attention. Whether we receive approval or reprimand, we seek the acknowledgment of those around us and we guide our behavior according to the attention-rewards issued by the those in our environment.

In any kind of rehearsal, practice, sectional, or even concert, from the student's perspective, what is the quickest way to gain your attention? By doing something positively or negatively? Which students are extended the most communication? Let's look one step beyond: How does this exchange influence the entire group? Does it motivate the group to move forward, or does it deter the positive flow and hopeful expectations of the all-too-short rehearsal period?

For the sake of example, let's say that the quickest way to gain attention in most cases would be to do something wrong. Misbehaving, talking during class, being rude, interfering with another student's performance, not paying attention, and a host of other choices are almost certain attention-getters. Teachers with every good intention of clearing up the problem may bring the entire group to a standstill while explaining the inappropriateness of the behavior of the guilty party.

Haven't we all walked out of the rehearsal in a state of frustration, trying to justify our actions (or reactions) to a situation which not only prevented any musical improvement, but set the group back three rehearsals? Of course, we then have to deal with the emotional residue which is certain to soil all those in the ensemble. When all is said and done, our actions are usually based on where we, as educators/directors, focus our attention.

Logic would suggest that we ignore the students' negative behaviors and acknowledge their positive contributions. However, any accomplished musician is well aware of the fact that the job is to "correct what is wrong." (Remove the clams, if you will.) How is this possible if we ignore the things which are wrong? The skeptic immediately visualizes one of those shallow rehearsals where the students are given a false impression of their achievements and contributions by a flood of undeserved compliments. Rest assured, this kind of teaching technique would guarantee the demise of any organization. It would be analogous to watering weeds in a garden. Eventually the weeds would consume the flowers.

The other end of the spectrum is the all-too-familiar rehearsal environment based on fear. The conditions are as restrictive as the personal resistance to the confining demands. This tension can be felt in the musical performance: ice cold and squeaky clean—the consequence of an atmosphere where control and dominance have replaced freedom and creativity. The musicians are programmed and conditioned to do only what they have been told to do—no more, no less. Research indicates these students have difficulties progressing without the detailed instruction of the director and are hesitant to take any initiative or venture outside the "safety zone" because of the possible repercussions.

Both of these scenarios create a less-than-ideal growth experience for either the director or the students. We all desire the value of group discipline, yet we encourage our young people to reach beyond their present limits and explore their growth potential and talents. Is there some way to have the best of both worlds? Can we guide the students to take risks and investigate new realms of expression without losing control of the group's ultimate goal? Emphatically, *yes!*

Behavior modification is nothing more than a stimulus-response process. We repeat any behavior for which we are rewarded. In this case, the reward would be your *attention*. The students who are given the greatest amount of your attention literally determine the dominant attitude of the group. They are the ones receiving the greatest rewards for their behavior—and others will modify their actions to be in line for their fair share of the bounty. Add this proven truth to the next bit of leadership understanding and new horizons appear: *criticize in private, praise in public.*

CRITICIZE IN PRIVATE. If there is a need for an adjustment in the behavior or attitude of a student, meet with the pupil privately. Privacy will afford a candid exchange without the entire ensemble serving as a judgmental audience. The rehearsal time can be spent dedicated to rehearsal.

One of the healthy byproducts of this scenario is the respect the students gain for you and the professionalism of your teaching methods. When we can avoid the emotional-ism often associated with critical admonishment, everyone benefits. Developing this habit may take some strict personal control, but the advantages are beyond measure.

This approach does not preclude those times when we simply need to have everyone put their music down to have a good old-fashioned heart-to-heart. Such times can be some of the most inspiring and focusing learning adventures in our musical growth. However, they must be used sparingly or they will lose their impact and become one of those "here we go again" lectures. (How many times did the young boy cry, "Wolf!"?)

PRAISE IN PUBLIC. This could well be the key ingredient. How often do we stop a group and publicly praise a student or a section's fine work? Do we ever simply thank them for being on time and having their instruments and music ready, or for taking the time to mark their part following a sugges-tion? Have we ever made a "big deal" out of the students who took it upon themselves to have an unscheduled section-al? Is there much taken for granted and little *attention* given to the faithful majority who go the extra mile to be on our bandwagon? Are there many opportunities to reward various students for positive contributions, or are our energies always directed to the negative few? These are difficult ques-tions, but the answers can lead us to optimistic and profitable behavior modification, fostering a new path to better rehearsals, performances, and overall attitude of everyone involved.

The field of music education offers a challenge like none other. The quest for the elusive "perfection" has caused even the most talented to shake their heads in dismay. In truth, any great musician knows that the assigned goal is only another step towards a higher level of performance and understanding. The development of habits through the process *is* the means to the end. Therefore, in bringing our groups to a higher level, we must dwell on the process (rehearsals, communications, etc.) through an effective means of behavior modification. When we reach this goal, other new and exciting possibilities come into view which offer a new set of goals, etc., etc., ad infinitum.

Never be satisfied with reaching a goal. Once you have reached it, savor it briefly and then move toward your next goal. If you stop there, you will stagnate. The journey toward the goal is much more rewarding than arriving at the destination.

Every musical garden (organization) will get attention. They deserve it, they demand it, and they will attain it to satisfy the human need. As educators, we have the wherewithal to determine which behavior to appropriately recognize and reward—and this is probably the single most important contribution we make to the child. When we choose to criticize in private and praise in public, we are opting to water the flowers while hoeing the weeds, a guaranteed technique for a superior musical garden.

"The art of teaching is the art of assisting discovery."
—*Mark Van Doren*

Being Instrumental in Opening Your Musical Possibilities

"How is the instrumentation of your group this year?"

That question can bring forth quite a response, but rarely do you hear someone reply, "Just fine except for the over-abundance of oboes and bassoons," or, "We just have too many clarinetists wanting to play bass and contrabass clarinet. And I feel terrible about the three harpists fighting over who can have the extra hour in the practice room."

For most, balanced instrumentation is an issue which needs constant attention, and even then it rarely results in the hoped-for outcome. So we go about substituting various parts, rewriting the solo for another instrument, converting (or coercing) a student into learning a new set of techniques to accommodate the called-for English horn part, etc., etc. All too often, directors simply throw up their hands in frustration and avoid any music which calls for specific instrumentation, or simply play the music with whatever instruments are available, possibly creating a void in the musical texture of the piece. In both cases, an injustice is done to the young musician. Case 1: The students never are exposed to some of the finest music written. Case 2: The students' understanding of what they rehearsed and performed is incomplete; it is not a fair representation of the composer's thoughts and ideas.

Another option, substitution, has been used effectively (and unknowingly) by many throughout the years. Even though the purist will denounce such a shortcut, it is a solution that seems better than either of the above options. One could argue that making substitutions ignores the ultimate responsibility directors have of balancing instrumentation, and it treats the symptom and not the problem. ("If we continue to settle for less than excellence, that is exactly what we will get; therefore, we must face the music and create the called-for instruments and accept nothing less than what is dictated by the composer.") This thinking is certainly valid, but if someone is not willing to put forth the kind of effort that such a goal requires, or does not even know the first step to take, the frightening alternative of "never exposing the students to some quality music" becomes the obvious answer to the dilemma.

We have long believed that it is a sacrilege to tamper with the creator's manuscript. *It's what the composer wanted, and who are we to doubt the pen of the artist?*" There isn't a music educator alive who hasn't asked him- or herself that question countless times. Although we all want to represent the music with as much integrity as possible, there may be some hidden benefits along the way which we have overlooked in our agenda of solutions.

Being a percussionist, I have spent many hours rummaging through music bins desperately trying to find music which matched the musical integrity level of the percussion students and would offer them a learning opportunity that would elevate their skills and demand the most of their talents. Fortunately, the percussion ensemble library has grown considerably over the years, but it is still far behind most of our fellow instruments. Perhaps in an effort to maintain a safe conservative posture as a percussion specialist, I ignored sharing with the students some of the most fantastic music ever written. Then, as an act of desperation back in the mid-70's, I took a huge risk and opened up a new galaxy of opportunities, as well as my own mind.

And so the story goes....

With a huge number of percussion "majors" at the university, we were running short on practice rooms, available instruments, lesson times, and above all, literature. Faced with musicians who could play the Goldenberg mallet method inside and out, and who were rather sick of more, and more...and more solo literature, it was obvious something "out of the present mode of thinking" had to come about or the momentum and enthusiasm of the group would begin to disappear.

My first thought was to simply sit down and write music; after all, I might as well put that composition degree to work. The time constraints, however, afforded little opportunity to spend the necessary hours at the manuscript paper. (And this was before our present-day music-writing computer programs were available.) One day as I was walking by the rehearsal hall, I heard some of the string players practicing diligently on a Mozart quartet.

I thought to myself, "How lucky they are to have an endless supply of quality music written for them by the masters. It's just too bad Amadeus didn't know about marimbas; maybe he would have written something for those of us who reside at the back of the musical bus. It's sad that most percussionists will never know how to tell their flutes to play a trill, for the only time they address it is that one Rehearsal Techniques Class 101 during their second year in music school."

And then the light bulb finally went on: Why not transcribe a string quartet for mallet instruments? First violin could be the upper register of the xylophone, second violin could also be a xylophone—or the upper register of the marimba. The viola could be the middle range of the marimba, or perhaps even the vibes might play this part, and the cello part would be the lower octave of the marimba! *Yes!*

Though the first mallet quartet rehearsal was rough (mostly due to my bad manuscript), it brought about an excitement which had the halls buzzing with the good news. A new potential had been unlocked and everyone was rushing to take part. Then someone pointed out that really no transcribing was necessary; the parts could be read as printed and the person playing the viola part would simply have to read the viola clef. The clef was taught as part of string class anyway, and here was a pragmatic way to put that knowledge to use.

The boundaries became endless. Students ran to the jazz band library and began to rewrite saxophone and trumpet parts in a new key. They raided the concert band library and the percussion folders quickly began to expand with more and more student transcriptions. And just before the Christmas holidays *to what our wondering eyes did appear?*...but the parts and score to the *Nutcracker Suite* transcribed for percussion ensemble. The challenge was met with an enthusiastic commitment.

Though there were many skeptics filling the recital hall that December evening, the concert ended with a resounding ovation as eighteen percussionists captured the inquisitive ears of a packed auditorium. Even the most critical audience members agreed the concert was something quite special!

Admittedly, there were moments when I thought the muses would strike us down for assuming any artistic right to alter the classics, but after witnessing the musical growth of the students, it would have been worth the confrontation. The students became hungry to learn more about the composers and their music—usually only a brief part of the percussionist's curriculum. Playing a few timpani notes while the orchestra is digging into Brahms is not the same as playing Brahms, particularly when the director's instructions are typically, "Percussion, you don't have to come to rehearsal until Thursday. You have no parts until the last movement."

No, music for string quartets does not sound the same played on mallet instruments. Yes, there are probably many nuances lost in the transition. No, the texture doesn't afford the same musical tapestry as violins, violas, and cellos. Yes, it does take some imagination to adapt the cello parts. *But it still exposes the player to the genius of the composer.* The phrases are still there. The cadence and musical thoughts are still in the notes. The performer still experiences the joy of painting the aural picture. The chance to get inside one's soul with the music is still possible.

If we could ask Mozart's permission to adapt his work to other instruments, do you think he would say no? I hope not, and I doubt it. Although it appears we are trespassing, are we simply not borrowing on the brilliance of a prodigy and allowing others to take part in that brilliance?

The above scenario is the extreme of adaptation. It is nothing like substituting a piano for a celesta, or a synthesizer for a harp, or even a xylophone for a piccolo. However, at the discretion of the conductor, it seems crucial that we bring the finest music possible to those students who are in front of us and anxious to perform quality literature. If it means making some calculated substitutions, then it appears to be in the best interest of all concerned.

The destination must always be to achieve the perfect instrumentation, while the journey has to focus on teaching music through quality literature. Even winning coaches make substitutions during the game!

"To be always intending to live a new life, but never find time to set about it...this is as if a man should put off eating and drinking from one day to another till he be starved and destroyed."
—Sir Walter Scott

Time Management Equals a Successful Music Program

In the world of band directing, there is never a "down time." Band directors are the first to start the academic year (with pre-school band camp) and are often the last to finish (performing for the graduation ceremonies). Then there are those who participate in a summer band program, the traditional band camp crusades, concerts in the park, Fourth of July parades, and a host of other community events.

Even athletes have seasons: football in the fall, basketball during the winter, baseball and track in the spring, and so on. Most of the time each team has its own coach. Yet for most band directors the expectation is equal to, if not greater than, the most active of varsity sports...and it goes all year long!

We are not here to decide whether this is right or wrong; that is an issue which can be argued another time. Instead, let us deal with the reality of "what is" and focus on teaching music as the top priority of the often overcrowded calendar. Unfortunately, the demanding performance schedule often becomes the tail which wags the dog. An overwhelmed director simply survives from one event to the next, silently praying for a few days of respite to regroup. But even when this supposed break does show up, it quickly disappears and the performance treadmill once again takes over, running at top speed, demanding that every hour be committed to seemingly every requisite except teaching music.

The frustration increases, desperation sets in, choices are based on survival instead of values, and the predictable pattern for burnout is in place. All energies are devoted to "Just getting through it," and any creative artistry is put on the back burner with a hopeful promise of "teaching music as soon as all the other stuff gets done!" This experience is a form of education which is well learned by the students (and the director) and, as one year is completed, many personal promises of the best intentions quickly give way to more of the same in the years ahead. It is much more comfortable simply to repeat past behavior than it is to re-establish a new system of teaching patterns. This once again confirms that the human is a creature of habits.

The above scenario does not have a happy ending. Eventually the young student musician or the director says, "Enough!" and simply gives up. Some quit, some stay but put forth no effort, and a few caring souls continue to run in the vicious circle headstrong in spirit but curious about where all of this leads and constantly asking themselves, Is it really worth the effort? The attrition rate in our school music programs is evidence of the severity of the problem. Educational budget cuts are causing administrators to aim the proverbial sharpened pencil directly at music. All of this simply adds more tension to the already stressed-out band director, and the professional fire continues to burn out of control, often fueled by the system itself. Isn't it time for a change?

• "But I'm just one person. What can I do to make a difference?"

• "I'm a music educator, not a trained lobbyist or negotiator. What possible impact could I have?"

• "You must be kidding! I don't have time to deal with all of this. Concert band festival is just around the corner, and I just had three of my first chair players quit. Can't you see I'm busy with important stuff!"

• "I know I should be more concerned, but right now we're in a fundraising drive for 150 new uniforms, and I only have twelve of the seventy-one students in eighth-grade band signed up to come to the high school next year. We're busy making plywood-people to wear the new uniforms next fall."

• "How can you expect me to think about having a rehearsal dealing with music when we have two basketball games this week, a jazz band concert for the Rotary Club, a booster meeting, and solo-ensemble festival this weekend?"

Perhaps the answer is not a complete revamping of the whole organizational structure, but rather a better use of the time which is already available. The solution depends on a mutual decision with the students based on the premise: We are going to be more effective in our time management.

The following suggestions work only if there is an agreement between all the parties concerned. It may take a special meeting with the band and/or the officers to establish such an optimistic foundation, but the benefits are limitless. Once the students see what there is to gain, they will quickly adopt the proposals and begin to utilize them, enjoying the exciting results of the agreed-upon plan. Certainly it is important the students "own" this collective blueprint of future musical prosperity.

1. START REHEARSALS ON TIME. When the bell

rings, let's be in the seats, properly warmed-up, and ready to begin making music. All too often, time is lost while simply getting people in their chairs with instruments in hand. There is a tendency to use pre-rehearsal time as an opportunity to socialize, and this activity has no time restraints. Then comes the predictable lecture from the podium about wasting precious practice time, which, of course, takes up more time!

2. ESTABLISH AN ARTISTIC ATMOSPHERE. Because of the gregarious nature of the music students and the family-like situations which are established on trips to before- and after-school events, the habits of the social aspect of band can easily become transferred into the class. It must be clear that making music, whether it is practicing scales, working on a specific passage with one section of the band, or suggesting a new way to play a phrase, must be taken seriously. That certainly doesn't mean time spent making music has to be abusive or punitive, but instead is based on the reality that the joy of playing music comes from the continued progress and skill development.

3. COOPERATION BECOMES THE THEME OF THE BAND. Since much of our society is based on competition, students are quick to incorporate that same thought process into rehearsals. This creates a new agenda for energy focus. It must be made clear a band is inclusive. The purpose is not to be better than someone else, but to explore our musical potential together.

When the students (and director) are ready to embrace cooperation instead of competition, everyone steps forward and begins helping their fellow musicians. It is crucial to make the shift from an "I-me" attitude to a "we-us" attitude.

4. PRO-ACTIVE BEHAVIOR REPLACES REACTIVE

BEHAVIOR. Teachers can lose a great deal of time dealing with "reaction." Think of the number of hours which have been spent dealing with a student who has "reacted" to the outcome of an audition, the inconvenience of a scheduling conflict, a sarcastic comment by someone in the band, or a host of other situations which cause personal discomfort. Many band directors begin to spend more time counseling students than teaching music. (This is certainly not to suggest that these heart-to-heart talks are not important, but often these students are used to personal attention at the expense of the rehearsal time, holding the rest of the group hostage.) When a problem occurs, rather than "reacting," accept the situation and immediately go about seeking the solution with a "pro-active" frame of mind.

5. THE MAESTRO EFFECT. The successful band director will always establish a close rapport with the students. Over the years, the student/teacher relationship has certainly taken on a different flavor. Much of this stems from the many hours which everyone spends together, whether it is through extended bus rides to and from a concert, after-school practices for the musical, or taking part in the officer's meeting.

Today's students also are much more worldly in their approach to life because of their early entrance into the work force, the availability of a wide variety of subject matter on television, and the exposure to a high-tech society which demands quick results. What used to be the all-knowing professor communicating to the unknowing student has now become two people discussing the ramifications of a new world order based on a recent revolution or how to upgrade a personal computer in order to use a modem from home to office. (In both of those situations, the student could easily be more informed than the teacher.) This discussion is all well and good, but once the rehearsal begins, there must be a shift to the discipline patterns which have stood the test of time and served every great musical organization from the Chicago Symphony Orchestra to Hometown High School: *What the conductor says, goes.*

When this policy is in place it puts an important responsibility on everyone. The director *must* be prepared, and the students must "respond" accordingly. Someone must guide the boat while everyone else rows, trusting the helmsman is headed in a positive direction. The "maestro effect" will offer a new sense of purpose to the rehearsal and will nourish the musical growth of the ensemble.

As with any change of habits, it might be best to begin by adding one of the above suggestions at a time. The students will quickly experience a great deal of personal satisfaction, and they will begin to add their own new disciplines to the itinerary. This new flavor is exciting for everyone and can recharge a program which has been drained of the passion which is essential to making music.

There is nothing revolutionary or insightful about anything written here—it is simply a matter of taking the initial step of instituting the ideas and then monitoring the system and making course corrections along the way. Of course, such monitoring could well be the key to making everything we do more effective. Life works when we work.

"Until one is committed, there is hesitancy, the chance to draw back, always ineffectiveness. Concerning all acts of initiative and creation there is one elementary truth, the ignorance of which kills countless ideas and splendid plans: that moment one definitely commits oneself, then Providence moves too. All sorts of things occur to help one that would never otherwise have occurred. A whole stream of events issues from the decision, raising in one's favor all manner of unforeseen incidents and meetings and material assistance, which no man could have dreamed would have come his way. Whatever you can do or dream you can, begin it. Boldness has genius, power, and magic in it."
—W. H. Murray

You Make the Call

"It is easier to be better than somebody else than to be the best we can." It's a thought-provoking statement, isn't it? The following chapter is dedicated to all those who have judged, will judge (and you all will), and all who are faced with judgmental decisions.

We may be asking more of the adjudicator than is humanly possible, and in the endless search to find the elusive "winner," we have lost the real value of the judge's contribution.

The world of adjudication is one which is difficult to explain. We have come to think that art needs to be judged and, therefore, have devised different systems to put art in its proper order.

Music is not the only area which has been subjected to this procedure. From the Academy Awards to the local talent show, everyone wants to know who won. Who is the all-time champion? Why didn't we get first place?

Unfortunately, we have tried to liken our art form (music) to the athletic world via a competitive arena to come up with the finite answer: Who really is the best?

If we as educators are not cautious, some serious problems are certain to arise. To be exact, we allow the "results" of the judges' decisions to take precedence over the performance itself. In other words, we become more concerned with the adjudicator's opinions than we do the concert, solo, recital, or whatever the context of the artists' creations. The cart is before the horse, the gun is fired and then aimed, etc.

The minute we add some form of adjudication to the forum, we also add the element of competition and an agenda of predictable questions are inevitable:

• Can, or should, we rank and rate a musical performance?

• Who is really qualified to make this judgment?

• How do we react in a positive manner when we do not agree with the judge?

• Can we really compare Mozart to Andrew Lloyd Webber?

• What educational value can we gain from this procedure?

Not only are these questions important, but the contrived answers may only be treating the symptom and not the problem. The real question is, *Can we, or should we, judge music?*

If your answer is no, than you simply don't involve yourself. If your answer is yes, sometimes, maybe, or anything other than no, it demands further inquiry to educationally justify the participation of your students.

Competition is certainly a part of our society. Our political system is built on the premise of free enterprise. How many times have we all heard this pre-contest phrase, "May the best man win"? To ignore the predominance of competition would be naive, but to think we can really pick a winner in the field of music or art may be just as blind.

Unfortunately, we all have known people who devote their lives to winning trophies, only to find they have become addicted to the process. In this scenario the extrinsic victories become more important than the intrinsic satisfaction of exploring the endless world of musical expression.

Though it feeds the ego of the successful player, it is suicidal for the participants/students; if per chance they do happen to come in first, all is fine, but if they fall short (based on some judge's opinion), it can be a devastating experience, often leading to avoidance (quitting) rather than reinvesting more time and energy.

The reason for throwing in the towel is based on a logic which is generated from the competition arena itself—*Why try if I can't in? It would be stupid to work this hard only to fall short and have to live through this embarrassing disappointment again.*

Haven't we all arrived at similar conclusions in our lives? We know society cheers for the underdog but chums up to the top dog. That being the case, why should we purposely gamble on putting ourselves in a less-than-attractive posture? It is much less painful to not try than to try and fail.

Let us suppose the competition arena is not the problem, but rather the difficulty lies in the interpretations of the results of the event. Please understand, I'm not suggesting we take away the desire for excellence or the self-discipline required to achieve high levels of quality. Those are the benefits of competition: the strengthening of the individual while honing personal skills for greater self-improvement.

If we choose to participate, let us commit ourselves to being the very best we can possibly be and accept the responsibilities which go with this goal. (Let's play to win!) However, let's also shift the goal from the final outcome (the results) and refocus that energy on the preparation process.

If this is the priority, then the victory happens with each degree of improvement and is not in the hands of an individual judge who gets one chance to arrive at an opinion which translates into the judge's call. Shifting priorities is easy to talk about, but is quite different when we bring this formula into reality. It requires (demands!) a constant educational reinforcement of the concept for students, parents, administrators, community supporters, and all.

If one succeeds at this endeavor, then the contribution of the judging community takes on an entirely different aspect. We don't listen to the tapes or read the sheets with the idea of a defensive justification of the score. Instead, it becomes a vehicle to offer suggestions of what we can do to embellish the performance.

In essence, we become enthused about the "judge's opinion," for now it becomes fuel for growth. If there is validity in the data, then it can be used to advance the level of understanding. If we feel it is not valid information, we can dismiss it and move on. Most importantly, we do not have to get entangled in the game of numbers, but can use our energy to continue the endless journey of musical improvement.

It is a matter of perspective, isn't it? Being a very competitive individual, I have to constantly monitor my own approach. It is very satisfying to win and not so satisfying to lose, so the *win at all costs* option is always a temptation and the antithesis of that becomes *don't play if you can't win.*

But there is something of much greater importance involved in all of this. It is the educational responsibility we have to our students. Competition is a way we can bring people together to support and learn from others who share the same artistic interests. To make it anything more than that is self-deception. The value lies in the journey (participation) and not in the destination (results).

In recent years there has been an increased popularity in marathon races. The basic premise is not being number one, but rather, completing the race or pushing your own limits to new levels. There is something thrilling about watching a 75-year-old woman cross the finish line three hours behind the first-place runner, but the victory is still as satisfying.

As 10,000-plus runners line up for the 26-mile course, there is a spirit of cooperation and a genuine desire to help fellow runners when the going gets a bit rough. The bystanders cheer them on and offer cups of water, for they, too, want to play a part in the individual victories. The only way to lose in such a competition is to simply not participate.

The ultimate competition of life is with the person we see when we look in the mirror and the only way to win is by continuing to play the game to our best abilities. It is not a judge's opinion that determines our worth or artistic value, but rather our own opinion.

Certainly be wise about learning from other people's opinions and suggestions. Consider their thoughts and feelings and apply them where they are appropriate, but ultimately, *you make the call!*

"Nothing in the world can take the place of persistence. Talent will not; nothing is more common than unsuccessful men with talent. Genius will not; unrewarded genius is almost a proverb. Education alone will not; the world is full of educated derelicts. Persistence and determination alone are omnipotent."
—*Teddy Roosevelt*

Proper Care and Feeding of Music Boosters

Today's music educator might not exist if public schools eliminated booster organizations. We would definitely see a shift in the curriculum to exclude many of the "taken-for-granteds" which sustain bands (and any school performing group) as we know them today: travel, additional teaching staff, audio-visual equipment, instruments, uniforms and proper concert attire, and immeasurable nutrition offered in the form of potluck dinners and annual chili suppers. Life without boosters is difficult to envision, isn't it? It's a bit frightening, also.

Parent booster organizations are as much a part of the foundation of any fine band program as the B-flat scale. Over the last two decades boosters have taken on a sophistication which has, for the most part, served the band community well. Suffice it to say they have become more than just a "booster" organization—they are an integral component to the health and welfare of a thriving band program.

When asked, "Why do you have a parent-booster organization?" many directors are quick to reply, "To raise money for the band." There is no doubt this is part of the agenda for the group, but perhaps there is much more to it. Let's take a look at this whole concept from another angle. To borrow a phrase from John F. Kennedy, instead of asking, "What can the booster club do for us?", it may be time to ask, "What can we do for our boosters?"

All too often, we see boosters as nothing more than fundraisers: they make money, the band director spends it. When the money is all spent, the boosters raise more money to spend...and the proverbial theme goes on until finally the goose that lays the golden egg either dies or quits coming back to the nest.

The astute music educator is well aware of this selfish hazard and begins to create other assignments for the proud parents. There are certainly many avenues of *boosting* which will serve everyone in a more positive fashion, and they do not cost money, but create a community of dedicated and committed band fanatics who will be eager to raise the required money when it is needed. *There's more to it than money!*

Everyone enjoys being recognized, acknowledged, and appreciated for their involvement. The key to making this happen is through meaningful and frequent communication. Here are some ideas which can serve as a starting point for those who are genuinely interested in having a booster organization which is based on a common goal of *the development of the child through musical excellence.*

BENEFITS FOR BOOSTERS

ATTENDANCE AT EVENTS. We all know mom and dad

are still the most important audience to the young performer. Unfortunately, with today's busy schedule, many parents do not attend the performances. With a personal letter of invitation, this trend might be reversed. A computer-wise student or an excited band parent could well serve as the source for a one page letter including an update of the band's progress, a reminder of the upcoming performance, and some healthy persuasion to attend in support of their child. Attendance will also improve if certain parents are recognized during the concert. Booster names on the back of the concert program can also serve as a draw. In addition, a reception following the concert creates an opportunity to set up new communications. Make it an important occasion, one the parents can't afford to miss.

Let's not forget the popular "phone tree." A personal phone call is certain to bring attention to the upcoming concert date, and it also offers a chance for conversation about the band. Can there ever be enough of this word-of-mouth advertising?

BOOSTER BANQUET. We have traditionally held the annual band banquet for the students. Why not have the band organize a thank-you dinner for the boosters? Use this as an occasion to showcase various ensembles throughout the evening and extend special recognition to the booster officers, patrons, contributors, etc. Present all those who attend with a certificate of appreciation and put the spotlight on those people who have gone the extra mile on behalf of the program. Make it fashionable to become one of the booster members. This is a perfect chance to involve administrators and community officials. Can you imagine what it will mean to the students to be able to be involved in this kind of appreciation evening?

Ambitious directors can also add an evening of dancing

with the jazz band providing the music. You will start an annual affair which will bring people out of the woodwork.

SUPER BOOSTER MEETINGS...THE PLACE TO BE. Time is such a precious commodity in our modern day world. Nobody wants to spend their free time in the middle of a meeting which is going nowhere. Plan as much of the meeting as possible in advance with the executive council. Give the meeting a voting agenda with a limited amount of time devoted to discussion. Avoid allowing the meeting to become a stage of opinion expression—all of that can be handled in various committees. Instead, spice up the gathering with some live background music as the parents arrive. (Here's a place to use that clarinet quartet or flute trio—they need the exposure as they prepare for the local ensemble festival. Save the percussion ensemble for the end!) Schedule a short welcome by one of the school officials. It is always appropriate to have one of the students speak to the group for five minutes to explain what is happening in the program.

Instead of the booster meeting being a dreaded necessity for all concerned (including the band director), use the time as an eagerly awaited stage to let people know about the positive growth and development of the program. It's hard to vote "no" on any proposal which is going to benefit the stars of the show.

BOOSTER THANK-YOU CARDS. The school print shop or a local band patron who owns a stationery store can have thank-you cards printed with the band logo. There are always countless parents who deserve an extra pat on the back for their efforts. With some guidance and careful planning, the band students can send handwritten notes of appreciation to these valuable boosters. This project has a win-win implication. Not only does it accomplish important communication with the band parent, it also creates a priceless learning experience for the students involved and reinforces the exchange-sharing between the boosters and the band personnel.

A GIFT FOR ALL SEASONS...AND REASONS. At some point in the year, it would be advantageous to have an appreciation gift of band memorabilia sent to the house of each booster. No, don't send it home with their own child, but have one of the other band members deliver it with a few kind words of acknowledgment. Use this as a chance to send along a schedule of the upcoming events and any other band news that is pertinent. This type of personal touch is not only a lost art in today's hectic world, it's also the most genuine way of expressing gratefulness. Suggestions could range from a tape of the band's performance, a photo calendar with the band on the front, a huge thank-you card with handwritten messages from the students, etc. The options are endless, inexpensive, and the seeds for a successful future of booster participation.

LOOK TO THE FUTURE

We harvest what we plant. Those organizations which enjoy a successful band booster group are certain of this. It is to the advantage of the band to extend the band family and embrace the parents as an integral part of program. This concept in action is certain to give a *boost* to the entire band.

With a continuation of cutbacks from local and state governments, it is evident we must look to outside help to secure the positions of our music programs. The thriving bands of tomorrow are most certainly the ones who are building solid band booster organizations today. Continue to feed and care for the goose that lays the golden egg.

"You cannot fight against the future. Time is on our side."
—*William Ewart Gladstone*

High Tech vs. High Touch: The Best of Both Worlds

W*e've come a long way, baby,* or so it would seem. Look at all that "high-tech" has offered to make our musical programs more efficient and effective. What did people do before there were electronic tuning devices? Did people just go about playing out of tune? (Probably the only ones who were offended by the device were the small percentage of folks with perfect pitch.)

And what about all those amplifiers and synthesizers? How did those pre-historic jazz bands get by with those antiquated acoustical instruments? I'll bet those were boring cave dances.

Then there are the various echo-plexes, sound machines, string generators, tone distorters, octave activators, percussive duplicators, and we can't forget the electronic drum sets. (If Gene Krupa had only known!) We have arrived!

Let's not stop here, for when the rehearsals are done, we can pop in our twelve-tray-CD eight-million-watt equalizer deck, hooked to a stratospheric satellite dish, and beam in any one of six major symphony orchestras to give master classes to the beginning instrumental students. Each of the children will be armed with a 120,000-meg hard drive and billfold-size mainframe computer to record the lessons and properly store them for future reference. We're probably not far away from being able to invite, through teleportation, any world-class artist to join our ensemble for guest appearances by merely calling on the cellular phone mounted on our wrist watches, which immediately will trigger the Library of Congress (all on microchips by now of course) to send every student their assigned accompaniment parts via modem. This data will be altered into hard copy by personal fax machines built in as a standard feature of every instrument case.

At this point you may be laughing, crying, disgusted, or even appalled, but the high tech addicts know none of this is beyond the range of possibility, and much of it is presently within the grasp of today's technology.

There are two kinds of music educators in the profession: those who are exploring the world of high tech, and those who will. Learn it now, or learn it later, but there is no question that the benefits of being on the cutting edge are beyond measure. Most importantly, they will make teaching music more exciting for you and for the students.

Of course there is always the fear these new contraptions will violate the authenticity of the musical product. Can an electronic keyboard really sound like a celesta? The truth is, it takes a very discriminating ear to tell the difference, and even that distinction may need the help of two observant eyes! Don't forget that the same electronic keyboard can also replicate the sounds of a harpsichord or a bass marimba and everything in between. (Shall we compare the cost of one synthesizer to the battery of "real" instruments needed to produce the same musical timbre? The purists better have a big budget.)

Though it is difficult to let go of our cherished disciplines and favored traditions, perhaps we can rescue the best of the old and blend it into an acceptable texture embracing the many pluses of high tech. We are living in an era of wonderful discoveries, and as stewards of the art of music, let's ride the crest of the wave and bring forward what our forebears gave us to join the magic of today's inventions. Music is a vehicle of expressive communication; why should we restrict it to a limited source of possibilities? At this point in time, the conservative music educator with a staunch attitude of denial could be following in the path of the dinosaur.

Certainly this is not to suggest that we dismiss everything we have. Let's not quit demanding fine tuba virtuosity simply because we have an electric bass as a possible substitute. Rather, we should use the available high tech to embellish what already exists. If the performance group is playing a transcription that calls for a harp and none is available, it seems logical to simply flip the synthesizer to "harp mode" and enjoy the composer's intentions, rather than to go without this addition simply because it might be impure.

If nothing else, let's not turn our back on the masterful organizational time saver, the computer. No more card files, incomplete ledgers, lost budget folders, inaccurate class lists, misplaced calendars, etc. Everything is at your fingertips. (Be sure to read the page on "backing up" the data!) Instead of spending countless hours hand-addressing every envelope, the computer can print and sort all the names and addresses while you teach a clarinet sectional. Music can be ordered from your desk without even picking up a pen. Questions about every aspect of the program can be sent out on the network and a multitude of answers will be waiting for you "on line" after your booster parent meeting. If you don't have a computer, get one. If you do, continue to learn more about it. Computers are no longer a luxury—they are a necessity if you are truly interested in saving time so you can educate instead of wasting precious minutes doing boring clerical work. A computer can do it much better than you and without a hint of emotional struggle. (Again, don't forget to read the section on "backing up" your files, or your entire life will be backed-up!)

This high tech stuff is pretty slick, except it cannot replace *you*. They have yet to invent some battery-operated device that can tell a young person that she is an important part of the group. Only the teacher can pat students on the back or bathe them with a warm smile of appreciation. There is yet to be a computer chip that can express "feeling," and after all, that is what music is about: *the expression of feeling.* What all of these boxes of wires and plugs bring to us is the opportunity to spend more time sharing the human element of the art and less time devoting the most important instrument of all, the mind, to mindless activities.

When you walk into the rehearsal room and turn on the lights, do you think, "If Ben Franklin had minded his own business, we wouldn't have to put up with these artificial suns!"? When your telephone rings, do you admonish that culprit, Alexander Graham Bell, for the inconvenience this tool of the devil has brought to your daily life? Wouldn't you rather take the group on a trip in Conestoga wagons rather than those luxurious busses with videotape machines and rest room facilities?

But these examples are different, aren't they? Not really. We have just come to take them for granted, just as the next generation will look at us and wonder why we ever resisted pagers, laser operations, space travel, and a host of other high tech contributions.

We are all a bit hesitant to try anything new, different, unknown, or out of our comfort zone, but that is the very place where dreams become realities. Somehow we think this means we might no longer be needed, wanted, or have anything worthwhile to contribute, but the reality is just the opposite. High tech opens the way for us to engender more passion, more sentiment, more emotion, more of who we are into every aspect of our teaching. It frees us to be students and teachers at the same time, to humble ourselves as we learn and grow, and to empower ourselves and our students in the process.

So let's turn on the juice and strike up the band.

"The man that hath no music in himself,
nor is not moved with concord of sweet sounds,
is fit for reasons, stratagems and spoils;
The motions of his spirit are dull as night,
and his affections dark as Erebus:
Let no such man be trusted."
—William Shakespeare
The Merchant of Venice

Visually Musical? Musically Visual? One in the Same

Having grown up in a world of visual musicality (my mother was a dancer), it always seemed obvious that sight and sound should intertwine as one expressive unit. To me, anything less suggested an amateur attempt at communication. Countless hours of observing mother create one tap-dance routine after another with the aid of her faithful RCA record player served as a solid base for writing marching band drills. The curriculum she offered was simple, without pretense, and as effective today as it was three decades ago: "You do not dance to the music, you *are* the music." Translated: "A successful visual program *is* the music." Or, as a friend once said, "If you can't hear the group, but know what music is being played by simply watching the show, you are witnessing the work of a true artist."

Watch a master choreographer at work. The process itself

is as thrilling as the final results. Bringing visual motion to the music offers a fascinating canvas of possibilities and an opportunity for the performers as well as the audience to enjoy a new level of understanding.

TIMES HAVE CHANGED.

Remember when the band marched down the field in a step-two pattern, played a pop tune for the majorettes, formed the school letters, and then exited the field triumphantly with the fight song to a standing ovation with the fans clapping in time and appropriately demonstrating their enthusiastic appreciation? Times have changed, haven't they?

The most dramatic difference, without argument, is the visual aspect of the production. Visual musicality is the name of the game. Every aspect of the musical program has a rainbow of possibilities, including drill design, auxiliary, integration of various colors, body movement, field placement, instrument angles, and on, and on—far more than a down-the-field march which served us well for so many years. And with this exciting set of options comes added responsibilities for the director, including additional staff for rehearsals, an amended language for drill writing, a more critical selection of music, the coordination and administration of the various facets of the ensemble, etc. It is far more than a casual shift from the "good old days." In the midst of the added responsibilities, it is easy to get so deeply involved in the various aspects of the program that the final production becomes a potpourri of segmented ideas rather than a unified musical-visual creation.

How does one avoid this all-too-common pitfall?

Is there a key to success which should be used while writing?

Can we be certain the end result will reflect the invested

efforts?

Does the visual program match the musical program? Though the last question sounds almost too simplistic, it unfailingly leads one in the right direction (or keeps one from continuing in the wrong direction).

Stand back, watch, and listen. Ask the performers if the visuals "feel right" with the music. If there is a musical climax without visual support, make the necessary adaptations. If the color guard has some spectacular move, but it does not coordinate with the music, take the opportunity to add appropriate percussion parts to emphasize the impact.

In other words, don't allow yourself to get so entangled in the logistics and administration that you do not take time to draw upon your most valuable tool: *your artistic talent.* Use the countless "effects" at your disposal to more clearly communicate the music, and if it is appropriate and called for, you also can add musical "effects" to give greater audio dynamics to the visual panorama.

Too often, we do not see the finished product until the actual performance. Then we stand in embarrassed disbelief as a helpful colleague points out the obvious mismatches in the visual musicality. Our rationalization is weak, at best, for we also see the fallacy of our shortcomings. This is a self-victimizing situation which is easily avoided if we continue to ask ourselves, Does this fit? As a general rule, if something is forced or needs to be defended, it is not right. Let us not wait until the final run-through to bring this question to the table. The dialog should be ongoing with each added piece of the puzzle.

BEFORE YOU DO ANYTHING ELSE...

The urgency to "get the show on the field" often violates any chance of artistic endeavor. With tight schedules and limited rehearsal time, the priorities often point towards *com-*

pletion instead of *creation*—and at the expense of the performers, audience, and overall program. Take a hint from the pros: know (feel) the music inside and out before the pencil hits the charting paper. Sketch to the music, move to the music, envision the colors of the music, sense the texture, the tension and release points, the dynamic contrasts, the primary and secondary themes, the phrases, the entire personality of the musical score. Literally, *become the music.*

It is clear why mother never choreographed any dance without her preassigned, self-imposed 100 listenings. She often said it was then just a matter of putting on paper what she saw in her mind. Many of today's finest drill writers attest to this same fundamental discipline. In fact, one well-known designer told me, "After about forty or fifty times through the music, I can see the whole show in my mind like a videotape. Then it is merely matter of tracing it on the page so others can see it. That's the hard part for me. I wish I had a monitor for my mind."

EVERYONE HAS CREATIVE POTENTIAL.

Great performances are based on great writing/creation, regardless of the performance vehicle. We can all bring these opportunities to our students if we are willing to reach into the depths of our creativity, and there certainly are no short cuts to this beneficial end. Though many say they cannot adapt to the contemporary drill design, that would seem impossible for anyone who has graduated from college with a music degree. The only price one must pay for artistic license is time. Certainly, time is at a premium, but with car tape decks, Walkman recorders, and every stereo facility imaginable at our fingertips, we can get in our "listening" while doing a myriad of domestic chores, traveling from one destination to another, or even sharing the music with our students. (Do they "see" what we see?)

Creative people are people who believe they are creative. It is a matter of choice. Though we are often impressed by the "quick genius" of many who seem to live in a world of instantaneous brilliance, the vast majority of artists are committed to the "process of creation," and are committed to a personal nose-to-the-grindstone formula for success.

THE BLANK CANVAS.

Ultimately, you hold the painter's brush. Enjoy the wonderful limitless possibilities of visual musicality and "Strike Up the Band!"

Part Three

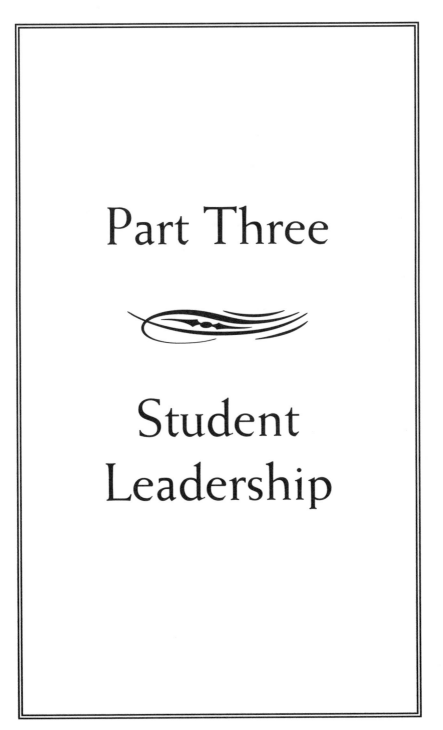

Student
Leadership

"I didn't say it would be fun, I said it would be worthwhile."

Student Leadership

W e know that our music students graduate to become leaders in all facets of society. When we challenge them with the proverbial phrase "You will be the leaders of tomorrow," we speak the truth.

Over the years one of the greatest challenges of my workshops has been to convince students of the personal sacrifice required to be an effective student leader. They are always eager to accept the benefits of the position, but often do not have a realistic understanding of what is expected. All too often, they see student leadership as a political attainment rather than a commitment of personal time and effort to a higher level of responsibility. Unfortunately, they rarely understand others (their followers) are going to feel the impact of their actions and they must behave accordingly and be willing to extend themselves more than their peers.

Student leaders are often selected because of their musical talents or performance skills. Because they sing or play well, we assume they will be a positive role model for their peers. This isn't necessarily the case. Leadership is about dealing with people. It involves communication, developing trust, supporting the followers, creating goals and plans, completing those goals and plans, and a host of personal skills that demand the ultimate in self-discipline. It means choosing the road less traveled, going the extra mile, giving up giving up.

It is easy to understand why many teachers avoid using student leaders. It requires a separate curriculum and, as we have all heard many times, *if you want it done right, do it yourself.* However, if we are preparing our young people to face the responsibilities of life, what better atmosphere to give this training than the music program, which is a microcosm of their world ahead. Developing a program of student leadership demands more involvement from you, the teacher. Of course, during that process, everyone (including the teacher) learns. It is the ultimate win-win situation.

As a basic theme, we must constantly remind our students: leaders enable people rather than encumber them. Leadership is an action verb. There can be no leadership without action, so lead, follow, or get out of the way.

"We find the greatest joy, not in getting, but in expressing what we are. Men do not really live for honors or for pay; their gladness is not in the taking and holding, but in the doing, the striving, the building, the living. It is a higher joy to teach than to be taught. It is good to get justice, but better to do it; fun to have things, but more fun to make them. The happy man is he who lives the life, not for the honors it may bring, but for the life itself."
—*R. J. Baughan*

Personality Traits of the Effective Student Leader

Did successful programs create the importance of student leadership, or did the importance of student leadership create successful programs? Which came first, the chicken or the egg?

Perhaps the answer to the first question doesn't matter; what does matter is the reality that thriving music education programs have developed a very sophisticated structure involving students at every level of responsibility. Whether out of necessity or by design, the process is producing learning experiences which will benefit the participating students in every facet of life.

We have always known that school music ensembles represent a microcosm of society. One cannot participate in a band, choir, or orchestra and avoid the maturation skills that ensure successful behavioral patterns in adult living. Accepting the challenge to play an instrument in the ensemble or sing in the choir carries with it the certainty the individual will also be exposed to extended responsibilities, the need for self-discipline, advanced communication skills, and the importance of analyzing quickly and decisively. These are all fundamental qualities which serve as the basis of our educational system, to literally *prepare the student for life.*

Combining the student leadership role with the responsibilities of music is a winning formula for every young person who wishes to seize the opportunity. However, we must be cautious in our selection of the student leaders, for they will be required to fulfill all the expectations as a group member plus take on an agenda of additional assignments. All too often the initial enthusiasm gives way to the reality that student leadership means doing the work nobody else wants to do, dealing with uncomfortable personality problems within the group, or making seemingly unfair personal sacrifices. It is not always a pleasant journey, but it is definitely worthwhile and pays lifetime dividends.

Unfortunately, many students unknowingly accept leadership roles only to discover they are not willing, or do not have, the capacity to fulfill the assigned or implied requirements. Quite simply, they have bitten off more than they can chew. What could have been a very positive growth experience backfires, and the individual feels a sense of disappointment, anger, and frustration. Self-esteem begins to drop, uncertainty is ever present, insecurity replaces self-confidence, and the path of least resistance quickly becomes the most attractive option: quitting. In this scenario everyone loses—the student leader who now is in a worse position than prior to accepting the role, the followers who have been misled and often are cruel in their assessment of the leader's productivity level, and the teacher who has the responsibility of dealing with the wounded leader, the upset followers, and now has to find a replacement who can move the group forward.

To avoid this situation, let us look at some of the initial signs of maturation that indicate a student is ready for leadership. Students may also want to carefully review these fundamental requirements as they make their personal choices concerning future leadership positions.

INDEPENDENCE.

Seek the student who makes decisions on his or her own. Peer pressure will cause many to wait and see what their friends are going to do. These students are always "at the effect" of the group and being in agreement with their counterparts is more important than making a choice based on what they know will improve the situation. In many cases, the misbehaved student is one of the most potentially powerful leaders; it is merely a matter of turning the negative behavior into a positive pattern. These people are certainly independent, and their self-confidence is evident.

We respect independence. Our nation is founded on the very principles of independence. The basis of leadership is the ability to make the tough decisions independently.

SELF-WORTH.

Leadership can be lonely. Being a leader often means putting in extra time and energy with little attention paid to this "above-and-beyond-the-call-of-duty" effort. Although everyone enjoys the recognition of peers, it seldom is given. To expect to be acknowledged for every task a leader completes is simply naive. If the student leader's self-worth is based on the praise of the followers, then the reign will be short-lived. However, if the leader can move forward without the accolades of the followers, then the capacity for leadership grows.

Many leadership duties are mundane; they do not lend themselves to glamorous surroundings with a crew of enthusiastic followers ready to jump in and add their support. Though boring, these duties must be fulfilled and the leader will find personal satisfaction in completing the assignment knowing it will benefit the entire group. Gratification is not in the form of adulation from other group members, but in the realization that there is value in personal contribution. It is at this point the leader must draw upon his or her own self-worth.

PERSEVERANCE.

For many, the following phrase has become a leadership credo: *When the going gets tough, the tough get going.* Simplistic? Yes, but very true. There is no substitute for tenacity. A leader must give up giving up. There are certain to be many failures along the path of success. Those speed bumps of life must be seen as stepping stones to the goal. Without perseverance, the young leader will be tempted to give in and ultimately give up. In this case, all is lost. One of the distinctions between the leader and the follower is the tenacity required to continue while others have stopped.

Leaders will face incompetence, ignorance, ineptitude, fear, and a host of other uncomfortable labels. It is at this junction where the true leader steps forward and takes charge. Instead of reacting to the situation and retreating to a safer position, the leader begins the task of solving the problems at hand. There is never a question of turning back, but simply finding the most effective way of moving forward.

Independence, self-worth, and *perseverance* are key factors in identifying student leaders. These attributes can be seen in students through class behavior, personal habits, and responses to various circumstances. It is crucial we carefully select these people, for they will have an impact—either positive or negative—on all those they lead, and most definitely on the entire program. It is important to remind our student leaders of the universal law of leadership: *You can't lead others until you lead yourself.*

We are careful in our audition process to make certain the right person is assigned the appropriate part to guarantee musical success. That same discretion should be applied to the selection and assignment of student leaders. The performance of the group offstage will reflect the success of the group onstage, and much of this will be determined by the effectiveness of the student leaders.

"A teacher affects eternity;
he can never tell where his influence stops."
—Henry Brooks Adams

Silence Is Golden

The following chapter was written for the entire instrumental ensemble and the appropriate discipline needed to attain a high level of performance excellence. Of all the instruments within the ensemble, this chapter may be best suited for my fellow percussionists.

"Drummer jokes" are as common to the band world as valve oil, and the theme of the humor (?) usually revolves around the irresponsibility of the young musicians.

Since music often requires an expertise in "counting rests," the percussionists may find themselves faced with an extended period of "silence" and little opportunity to play the dictated percussion instrument. Idle hands are the devil's plaything. With that in mind, the following words may serve as a positive road map for future rehearsals and performances.

In defense of my compatriots, we are not often instructed as to "the expected behavior" in a six-minute composition that requires extensive counting and a three-measure suspended cymbal roll. With the knowledge and understanding of what will benefit the entire ensemble, the percussion section can transform the moments of "silence" into something very special for all of the band.

As my dear friend Gary Green, Director of Bands at the University of Miami, said, "There can be no music without silence." With that in mind, let us quietly move on....

"Playing Rests"

It sounds silly, doesn't it? One doesn't play rests, one rests during rests! It would be more appropriate to say "one doesn't play one's instrument during the rests, but one does *not* take a mental vacation either!" It is a matter of semantics for the most part, and certainly something few of us address in our rehearsals, let alone performances.

Consider your own rehearsals, whatever the musical group: Do you not find all of the discipline problems and annoyances happening when the individual or section is musically tacet and behaviorally double forte? How many times have we all used these familiar quotes: "Flutes, will you not whisper during the oboe solo!" "Why are the third clarinets passing written notes?" "Pay attention to me!" "Okay, which saxophone is responsible for this paper airplane? It has to be in the tenors, because the altos were playing...anyway, the fuselage is made from a chipped tenor reed!"

"French horns, who gave you permission to write letters during the second movement?" "Trumpets, if you would not talk during the rests, you would know when to come in! And quit trading mouthpieces and tuning slides!" "That's it, trombones! Either you quit squirting each other with the water bottles or we go back to everybody playing in one position like the old days!" "Baritones, you are supposed to count rests, not play the first trumpet part by ear." "All right tubas, if I see any more food back there, I'm going to make you go back to auto repair class!" *"Drummers...sorry, percussionists* ...why is there a puppy in the equipment cabinet? Who's going to clean up this mess?"

Although we may be amused at these all-too-familiar statements, we know this is the very reason rehearsals bog down. By the time we recover from recognizing one of these incongruent behaviors, it has cost an untold amount of time, not to mention the complete destruction of any musical mood created up to that point.

As a percussionist, I have many personal experiences of sitting and standing through countless rehearsals without ever playing one note. The temptation to create some kind of outside interest was always dominant in my thinking...and more than likely manifested somewhere along the line. Results: a tongue-lashing from the conductor (often deserved) and a halt to the forward progress of the entire group—not to mention the personal agony suffered by the person behind the baton.

Think back to your times of guest-conducting and doing visitation clinics for your colleagues. Did you spend all your time working on intonation, phrasing, balance, and accidentals, or was some of it spent on deportment, musical attitude, and artistic conduct? Did any of your pleasantness turn into aggravation? Were you tempted to stop the whole rehearsal and express your thoughts about simple manners and common decency? If you didn't respond yes to at least one of these questions, many of us are interested in trading places with you.

Certainly this extraneous behavior on the part of the students is not generated to agitate the director of the organization (in most cases?). However, it comes from lack of knowing what to do during those 126 measure tacets. Few teachers told us anything about playing rests other than, "You're not supposed to be playing at letter B! Why are you playing? Can't you count?!"

Musicians must understand that everything they do during the performance (rehearsal) is part of the finished artistic product. One cannot escape or disappear, but must realize how he or she "fits into" the holistic spectrum and weave of the final product. In other words, "Get with the program!" The responsibility of the musician goes well beyond "Playing the right notes."

Visual images to the brain have a greater impact than audio data, assuming they are both at the same intensity level. Therefore, the beauty of a legato clarinet passage will be destroyed by a trumpet player falling off the back of the risers or a drummer signaling to his girlfriend in the alto sax section or a flute player fluffing the back of her hair. It's doubtful that any of these acts are a purposeful sabotage of the clarinets' "moment in the spotlight," but that is precisely the result. It serves as a diversion to everyone, even the clarinet section. (How often have we attended or conducted the elementary band's first concert and observed students waving to Mom, Dad, Grandma, Grandpa, etc.? *Too true!*)

The point is, we need to spend time talking about *how to play rests.* Part of being an all-around musician is understanding this important facet of performance. There are certain accepted behaviors, and to violate these standards and disciplines is just as costly to the group as playing wrong notes. When the proper "rest technique" is not part of the curriculum, you can expect to witness a new form of "creativity." Those rests will get played! Wouldn't you like to have some "artistic direction" on *how* they get played?

Most rehearsal time is spent working on details in the technical realm of the various instruments and, after all, that is our job: *to teach music.* We simply need to take into account that part of music is silence/rests. The attention to this particular detail will offer the conductor a fresh new approach to rehearsals and will, in fact, improve the rehearsals for everyone involved, not to mention the overall onstage (field) performance. Time gained through the focus of energy is remarkable, and the sense of pride instilled via the importance of each individual gives a new meaning and direction to the entire ensemble—even the percussionist who must count 256 measures for one triangle note!

We all have been well trained at teaching notes. Let us now explore the exciting world of teaching rests. *Silence is golden!*

ngly reinforce the I-me pattern of living, which is the
is of what we are striving to achieve in our musical
nity ("with unity"), opening the pathways to artistic
nces.

point is, as teachers, performers, conductors, and stu-
ve must constantly discipline our own behavior so it
ur actions with our desires. Consider having a Weight
s meeting at the local Baskin-Robbins—that would
ulous. If so, can we expect our musicians to offer a
el of cooperation in the rehearsal hall while the con-
s unwilling to make adjustments on a decision which
his/her personal desires? Granted, every situation
considered on its own particular circumstances, but
k at the overall question of program responsibility.
do you approach your conflicts of each day? Are you
as a role model and setting the standards you want
dents to emulate? Is your decision making in line
ur values of life? Do you ask of yourself what you
thers? If the answer is *yes,* then the rewards you
from everything you do will far exceed your greatest
ions. If the answer is *no,* it is time to review the why
choices and see if they are based on the we-us phi-
which is the fundamental theme of a quality pro-
erein lies a tremendous opportunity to bring a new
excitement to your group and to your own life.
ilbert Arland wrote, *"When an archer misses the
turns and looks for the fault within himself. Failure
e bull's-eye is never the fault of the target. To
your aim, improve yourself."* It is true that we can-
t the wind, but we can adjust the sails.
an have some say-so in the results because of our
, our willingness to cooperate, and our belief that
ave value simply because of who we are. And since
reatures of habit, we can assume that excellence is

*"I leave this notice on my door for each accustomed visitor:
'I am gone into the fields to take what this sweet hour yields;
reflection, you may come tomorrow,
sit by the fireside of sorrow.
You with the unpaid bill, despair,
you tiresome verse-reciter, care,
I will pay you in the grave, death will listen to your stave.
Expectations, too, be off! Today is for itself enough.'"*
—*Percy Bysshe Shelley*

I-Me vs. We-Us: A Look at Consistency

As musicians, our vernacular centers around
words and phrases like: ensemble, blend, focus, harmony,
unity, working together, responsibility, commitment, expression, creating an untried mood, bringing a sense of *oneness*
to the group, *espirit de corps*, etc. All of these thoughts are
generated from the fundamental philosophy that there is
more benefit for the individual through an emphasis on *we-
us* rather than *I-me.*

Certainly we would all agree that we do give up a good
measure of individuality when we become a part of a musical ensemble. We adjust everything from musical tastes to
living schedules to accommodate the end goal, the performance, the final product. The finest organizations we know
are those who set aside some of their "differences" for the

benefit of achieving a quality musical performance. Ultimately, everyone grows and learns because of the adjustment necessary in the group-goal endeavor.

This concept is nothing new. In fact, it is apparent in the classic poem "The Law of the Jungle." For those who have never read this enlightening piece of writing, indulge yourself:

"THE LAW OF THE JUNGLE"

Now here is the *Law of the Jungle*
and it's as true and as blue as the sky,
And those who obey it shall prosper,
But those who deny it shall die.

As the serpent who slithers the tree-trunk,
the law runneth forward and back:
The strength of the pack is each wolf,
but the strength of each wolf is the pack.

Simple, direct, insightful. We would all agree, wouldn't we? Although the radicals might scream an infringement of their "right to choose," the artist would claim this *is* the path to peak performances. It is the essence of the meaning of ensemble: striving for new heights of *unity, togetherness, oneness.*

It would be easy to simply add a concluding paragraph and claim another successful observation which brings new understandings to some, reinforces others, and offers a good lesson for the members of any musical ensemble. However, that would be too simple and really doesn't provoke much thought. It's just too safe. There is more to this which can serve as a challenge for all of us. On to the next level of thinking....

If the we-us philosophy is
excellence, should we not bring t
approach to every facet of life?
expectations, disciplines, or dem
ent with our behavioral styles?
tions seem so elementary they do
always amazes me that a cond
will convey one message with
for our *trust* in accomplishing
turn display an alternative attitud
mixed message creates some rat
It could well be a case of taking
steps backward. The survival pa
goes into action and the temptati
sive barriers for self-protection.
will be a goodly measure of "v
the rehearsal.

Do we not have the responsi
musical attitudes to our perso
musicians to extend themselves
tle serenity when they have just
back prior to rehearsal? If there
it has to come from the perfor
been destroyed somewhere al
chance it will appear in the mu
communication prevents the at
and prevents any opportunity
mance in music, not to mentic
other part of life.

Defensive actions, negative
ance of change, and stringent
from insecurity and/or fear. The
assume for self-protection. The
obstacles which prevent comr

and str
antithes
commu
experie
The
dents, v
aligns o
Watche
be ridic
high lev
ductor i
violates
must be
let's loo
How
serving
your st
with yo
ask of
receive
expectat
of your
losophy
gram. H
sense of
As G
mark, h
to hit t
improve
not dire
We a
approac
we do h
we are

not a part-time practice—it is not something we turn on and off; it is a way we approach everything we do and it begins to show up in each and every part of our life. Our *art* is a manifestation of who we are. Who we are will determine who our students will grow to be. This certainly goes well beyond the beginning and the end of a piece of music.

We all want the best for our students. We all desire to produce quality and make a positive impact on those around us. Nobody ever attains any real level of success by simply "doing what is required." Success comes from the amount of extra which is over and above the required. Therein lies the formula for greatness and distinction. We must constantly demand of ourselves what we expect of others. To improve our own conditions, we must embrace change instead of fear it, accept others and their insecurities, and love even those people who seem to disagree with our thoughts and feelings. This is not an end within itself, but an ongoing process. Security can be such a falsehood. Only those who are willing to admit their insecurities and shortcomings are truly secure. What a paradox!

The striving to achieve new levels of performance is far more important than the performance itself, for it ensures even greater performances to come. *Let the music begin.*

"My crown is my heart, not my head,
Nor decked with diamonds and Indian stones,
Nor to be seen: My crown is called content;
A crown it is, that seldom kings enjoy."
—William Shakespeare

Obeying the Three Laws of Student Leadership

Teachers take note: *Student leadership is no longer an option, it is a must.*

There is simply too much to do to assume you will have time to complete it single-handily. Certainly the parents can play an important role in the various responsibilities of the program, but the day-to-day operation of the group still comes back to those who are there at all times: the students.

After working with student leaders for more than a decade and developing an extensive curriculum focused on goal setting, communication techniques, time management skills, people skills, etc., it has become apparent none of this information has any value unless there is a fundamental understanding of what it takes to be a successful student leader.

There are many misconceptions which need to be cleared up before assigning the various tasks. For example, leadership is *not* about dominating another person. So often the students interpret their position as a license to verbally abuse or demean their peers. Nothing could be further from the truth. In fact, this is one of the quickest ways to violate the importance of the position and shut off the positive potential of everyone involved. (In this case, we would be better off without any student leadership.) Such a liability can be devastating. The focus must be on the forward progress of the group, not on pushing or threatening subordinates along the way. The emphasis must be on creating opportunities for others to grow, learn, and improve, literally *leading* them on a journey of personal advancement and achievement.

As you begin to choose your new leaders for the upcoming year, it will be to your advantage (and the welfare of the organization) if there is a purposeful understanding of three basic principles which are the key components of successful leadership. When these serve as the foundation for future building, you can feel confident about the positive possibilities ahead.

YOU CAN'T LEAD OTHERS UNTIL YOU LEAD YOURSELF.

This concept is crucial. It is an embellishment of the well-known phrase, *lead by example.* Role modeling is still the most effective leadership technique. It embraces all the peer pressure implications and offers a constant source of information to the follower.

Whenever there is a question or a decision concerning how to act or what to do, the follower can simply "watch the leader," see what is appropriate, and then model it.

Students imitate both positive and negative behaviors; therefore, the leader must be keenly aware of every predictable outcome based on how he or she acts in every situation. The followers will be close behind.

"Do as I say, not as I do" will be the certain downfall of any leader. One cannot show up late but expect the "followers" to be on time. The leader must establish the highest standards and then become the dedicated example of fulfilling the necessary requirements for goal attainment. As a leader, one cannot expect more from others than from oneself. As the engine determines the speed of the train, the leader dictates the responsibility level of the group.

Be certain the aspiring student leader is well aware of the number-one fundamental law of leadership. It is imperative this prerequisite be the basic theme. No exceptions.

YOU'RE ONLY WORTH WHAT YOU GIVE AWAY.

There are many talented and knowledgeable people who aspire to be student leaders. Unfortunately, they often are thrust into a position of authority based on their expertise, but find themselves ineffective in their ability to guide others. This results in frustration, abrasion, confrontation, and a total breakdown in communication.

Though talent and skill are vital elements in the selection of the leader, they represent only part of the competence-formula to guarantee effective leadership. Leaders must also "give away" or share the information with others.

A student leader who chides or berates another student because he or she cannot perform at the expected level or does not meet up to the talents of the "leader" is doing nothing to help the situation. It is less threatening for the subject of such chiding to withdraw than it is for that student to try again and not succeed. This logic is well known and creates a standstill for all concerned, including the leader.

Student leaders must be aware that personal risk is an important part of the agenda. Their leadership value is measured by their capacity to bring their knowledge to others, or in reality, to give it away.

YOU CAN ONLY GIVE WHAT YOU HAVE.

Though simplistic in reasoning, this premise is often overlooked because the student leaders are so busy with "what needs to be done." In an all-out effort to achieve the given goals, please the director, serve the followers, etc., the priorities become reset, and illusions of grandeur serve as the "leadership road map" instead of a realistic plan of action. Only in rare exceptions will the follower outperform the leader, and when that is the case, a new leader will soon be designated. Therefore, a program of ongoing self-improvement is required.

The equation is basic: *The more I have, the more I can give. The more I give, the more I learn, which creates more information to give.*

A very talented student will develop quickly, and the "new enthusiasm" will serve as high-powered fuel in the early-day stages of learning. Also take into account the student's desire to achieve a position of status within the band as well as the personal payoff which comes with the exploration of the art form. This observed motivation may *appear* to be the exemplary behavior model for the entire group, and there is a temptation to thrust this student into a high-profile position. Beware a common backlash of this hasty decision; the student often becomes enamored with the entrusted power and refocuses his or her energy into *self-promotion* instead of *self-improvement.* In other words, they give up their intense learning habits and become engrossed in personal advancement.

The chosen student must understand the leadership position carries with it the responsibility of *increasing* one's work ethic and establishing a new set of goals which reflect an even higher level of excellence and achievement. This requires a very mature understanding of what leadership commitment really means and is the distinguishing characteristic of the certain-to-be-successful student leader. There must be a dedicated program of continued learning to increase the value of the leader's message.

As you go about choosing your leaders for the future, it might be worthwhile to have them read this brief article and do a bit of soul-searching before deciding to throw their hat in the ring as a possible candidate. For the good of all concerned, let's be certain they understand and are willing to assume the responsibilities of what lies ahead.

It is counterproductive to have leaders who don't lead. If the leaders are patiently waiting for you, the director, to tell them what to do, then they are not leaders, but managers. *Managers do things right. Leaders do right things.*

When students observe the three basic laws of leadership:

1) You can't lead others until you lead yourself;

2) You are only worth what you give away; and

3) You can only give away what you have;

they will find themselves enjoying a feeling of personal self-worth, and everyone in the group will benefit from their productive and positive contribution. Take the lead!

"Thus only can you gain the secret isolated joy of the thinker; who knows that, a hundred years after he is dead and forgotten, men who never heard of him will be moving to the measure of his thought—the subtle rapture of a post-poned power, which the world knows not because it has no external trappings, but which to his prophetic vision is more real than that which commands an army."
—Oliver Wendell Holmes

Getting Serious about Being Positive

The title of this essay should provoke some questions in your mind. Isn't *positive* generally related with happy, upbeat, fun, or not negative? Although this is the popular premise, it is an incorrect interpretation and one, unless understood, which will keep many from any further exploration of the unlimited potential of the student.

Many educational researchers confirm that "a positive environment is the most conducive for maximum learning results." Immediately upon hearing this statement, our minds conjure up these visions of classes filled with frivolity and unrealistic happiness in a contrived situation overflowing with artificial sunshine—which we are certain is reserved for the carefully chosen study group and definitely is impossible in the realm of everyday teaching. Therefore, we dismiss the possibility of what a positive approach could mean to our students, our program, and ourselves and carelessly conclude it is impractical, idealistic, and has no application in the real world of music education.

Yet when we study the outstanding programs across the nation, there is one common theme: *Everything is based on a positive foundation.*

We have all heard the story about the young man who was diligently practicing his clarinet for the upcoming auditions. After several unsuccessful attempts to master his étude, he threw his instrument down and announced in disgust, "I'm going to really mess up on this playing test tomorrow!"

Jumping to his feet, his eager father reprimanded, "You must be positive!"

The aspiring young musician retorted, "You're right! I'm *positive* I'm going to really mess up on this playing test tomorrow!"

In this case, the young man was dealing with the essence of what positive is all about. On the other hand, his father was offering a weak (at best) solution to his son's predicament. Just "thinking" it is going to get better is self-deception at the highest level. (Remember the "Think Technique" from Meredith Wilson's *Music Man*?)

Our friend Webster defines *positive* as: *constituting a motion which is definite, unyielding, certain in its pattern; not fictitious; real, logically affirmative.*

Doesn't this also describe the attributes of a master teacher? Think about your most effective and influential mentors; didn't they bring these same positive traits to the learning process? Now let's go one step further and analyze our own teaching efforts:

• Do we constitute a definite forward motion?

Let's not confuse filling up time exchanging information as "definite forward motion." Although spontaneity is always a signature of a fine teacher, it must be above and beyond the careful planning of each day's goals.

• Are we unyielding and certain in our patterns?

When we settle for less than excellence, that's exactly what we get. It is important that our students understand our level of expectation. In truth, they do. Simply follow them from one class to the next and observe their behavior change according to the expectations of the teacher.

• Are we nonfictitious, real, logically affirmative?

We have all fallen into the trap of being unrealistic, much like the middle school band director who insists on playing a grade VI piece of music, or the private teacher who demands three hours of practice each day...or else! (Though we have fulfilled the non-yielding aspect of our positive definition, we have violated the "real" issue.) And when we address the area of "logically affirmative," we find this is the pivotal point of judgment which separates the good teachers from the positively great ones.

It is pointless (many think detrimental) to "affirm" anyone who has not accomplished the given task or assignment. That certainly doesn't mean we stop encouraging, inspiring, or supporting them, but we must be honest. Learn the fine art of correcting a person's efforts without damaging their self-image. To keep from hurting a student's feelings, we are often tempted to lower the standards so they will feel the accomplishment of the goal and as a result, raise their self-esteem. (This also means we do not have to confront the situation and the aftermath of emotion which comes with personal disappointment, so the path of least resistance seems to be an inviting option.)

Unfortunately, the short-lived pseudo-satisfaction is quickly replaced by the understanding that we shifted the rules in the middle of the game. This technique backfires and leaves the student with a sense of false security about the integrity of the original goals. (Remember when you were very young and played checkers with an adult who let you win? It is an empty feeling of self-doubt, isn't it?)

Conversely, when we fall short, but are met with the "affirmative logic" to immediately go back to the drawing board, hone our techniques and skills, and reach deeper into our creative potential—then the disappointment of not achieving the desired goal is replaced with the drive to try it again, knowing there will be a higher level of self-improvement which will honestly and positively raise one's self-esteem. Now that is positive teaching.

As we begin this new school year, we have new students, a new mix of personalities within our groups, and an opportunity to put some fresh new thoughts and ideas into practice. There is no second chance at a first impression. What better time to get serious about being positive?

"For of those to whom much is given, much is required. And when at some future date the high court of history sits in judgment on each of us, recording whether in our brief span of service we fulfilled our responsibilities to the state, our success or failure, in whatever office we hold, will be measured by the answers to four questions: First, were we truly men of courage.... Second, were we truly men of judgment.... Third, were we truly men of integrity.... Finally, were we truly men of dedication?"
—*John Fitzgerald Kennedy*

The Price of Leadership: Commitment!

Although this article will be focused on student leadership, the information is applicable to every person who is responsible to other individuals. That includes just about all of us, doesn't it?! There are very few tasks in life where one does not have to deal with, or be responsible to, another person. With that in mind, the whole study of "people skills" becomes of tremendous importance in terms of success at any level.

Volumes have been written about "leadership and management," and most have been directed to the corporate setting, yet much of the information can be tailored to the upcoming student leader, offering guidelines for a path to success for any aspiring seeker of excellence.

1. THE CERTAIN NEED. The day of one person "doing it all" is now a part of history. Certainly there are those isolated cases where Mr/s. Music Educator chooses to handle every detail from sorting music to counting the candy money, but the combination of tightened schedules, a full performance calendar, recruiting responsibilities, committee meetings, etc., have thrown a new light onto the situation. (Look back twenty years and see if the music programs of that day remotely resemble today's, i.e., yearly travel, expansion of athletic endeavors which can affect performance and rehearsal schedules, emphasis on fund-raising, the increased teenage "work force," music festivals at the local and national level, and on, and on. The demands on the time of a "music teacher" to also become a "music administrator" are obvious. This is not to say it is "good or bad," but simply "what is.")

There is a need for students to help complete some of the tasks at hand. This prevents the teacher (you) from spending countless hours sorting uniforms or making bus signs for the trip. (Even though both of those options might be more pleasant than the meeting with the booster club executive committee!)

2. THE DILEMMA. It is quite easy to select leaders to take charge of many of the projects to be done, but quite another thing to initiate, execute, and complete the assigned responsibilities. There is a "treacherous ravine of possible catastrophes" on this path of leadership effectiveness. It appears that most students are so enamored with "the title," they forget why there is a need for student leaders in the first place.

"A title does not a leader make." (We can certainly sight countless examples of this "mislabeling" in the adult world, can't we?!) So many student leaders interpret their position as "one of authority" where they will "tell others what to do and how it needs to be done." Nothing could be further from reality.

Although "delegation" is one of the four major leadership styles, it is reserved for the executive level of management, and even there must be used discreetly. For the most part, student leaders will be "leading by example." The student leader's work ethic combined with his or her chosen attitude will set the tone for those whom they will lead. (Perhaps a review of Tom Sawyer's classic fence-painting scenario would be an appropriate introductory story, assuming they will see the irony and continue to keep paint brush in hand!)

3. THE SOLUTION. In simple terms, the student must understand your expectations, and (prior to accepting the position) be willing to make a commitment based on that information. Of course, this increases the level of the game, for you must now reach into your visionary goals and clearly define what you want the student leaders to do; otherwise, these young people might as well be working on a jigsaw puzzle without seeing the final picture on the box!

The more specific you can make the information, the more chance of success everyone will enjoy. Continue to ask yourself as you prepare expectations for your leaders: Is it feasible? Is it explainable? Is it measurable? Is it necessary? In almost all cases, these "qualifiers" will tailor the task to the leader.

Caution: it is at this stage that many feel the preparation is completed and we're "off and running!" There is one more giant piece of the puzzle which is *absolutely necessary* if this student leadership picture is going to come into focus. Frankly, without it, the rest of this information is useless, and of course, this holds true for ourselves, too.

4. COMMITMENT. It serves as the mortar between all the "bricks of wisdom" and is most assuredly the one quality which separates those "who can" from those "who didn't." The student leaders must make a personal commitment to their assigned task. This "pledge of completion" is one of the most effective (and often overlooked) exercises in the leadership learning process. Once the mind accepts this charge, the chances for success are increased tenfold. The assignment/responsibility becomes a road map, and although there will certainly need to be course correction along the way, the destination is clear, the route is understood, and the individual is *mentally committed* to the completion of the journey.

The formula works if the student works.

We are now directly facing our relentless friend, *commitment*. And, of course, you cannot give someone commitment, but you can tell them what commitment is, what commitment takes, and the price commitment costs:

Commitment is what transforms a promise into reality. It is the words that speak boldly of your intentions, and the actions which speak louder than the words. It is making the time when there is none. Coming through time after time after time, year after year after year. Commitment is the stuff character is made of; the power to change the face of things. It is the daily triumph of integrity over skepticism.

It might not hurt to paste a copy of the above paragraph in every student's folder, not to mention on the walls of every classroom, and a few extra copies in the faculty lounge. The honesty of that short paragraph is the very essence which separates success from failure. Failure only happens when someone chooses to give up.

After countless leadership workshops stuffed with the

most up-to-date information, I find the success or failure of the "newly anointed leader" has little to do with the notebook of information (which is the same for every person in the room) or the examples sighted from successful leadership patterns, or even the hands-on assignments of the seminar curriculum.

In all cases, the potential leader is the one who is committed to getting the job done when it needs to be done, whether he or she wants to do it or not. They are committed to completion.

The power of a leader is measured by his or her ability to complete things.

In conclusion, it is exciting to work with student leaders because the patterns and habits they develop through this learning process will create a value system for every other facet of their life. *Success creates success.* The positive impact you are having on the student leader(s) is beyond measure. What greater gift can we bring to our students than the understanding of their potential? Here's the perfect opportunity! Take the lead!

"In life we learn that we, as individuals, are but a small part of a great whole...a fellowship, a family. As an individual we cannot grow or even survive without others. With this in mind we realize that no personal sacrifice is too great for the preservation of the group. We learn that the clamor of desires and ambitions within us must be silenced whenever they could damage the group. We find that we must consider the needs of others and not only ourselves. It is obvious that the group must survive or we as individuals will not."
—*Anonymous*

A Message to Students: How Does Your Band Live?

How does you band live? That's an unusual question, isn't it? We usually ask, "How does your band play?" But let's take this one step further and look at more than just the time when the instrument is in your hands.

Although we usually see the purpose of band as creating a fine performance, have you ever stopped to think that much of your "band time" is spent not rehearsing music? In many ways, band is like a big family, so it is important to look at that first question and really examine it, for the band experience will have an impact on your entire life.

Band is not like any other subject in school. Don't you act differently in band than you do in English or algebra, or even physical education? Do you find much of your life revolves around the band schedule? Just look at your normal school day and see how many times you are in or around the band facilities. Many people start out in the band room every morning; that is sort of the gathering place for all the band personnel prior to the first class. At some schools, all the band students have their lockers right outside the band hall and the between-class times is another chance to check in with all the band friends as everyone makes the proverbial "locker stop."

Have you ever requested a pass to leave a class and go down to the band room? Band students are infamous for skipping study halls and hibernating in the rehearsal room. And where does everyone meet after school? The band room! There's something different about band, and because of that, we need to address the important subject of *how your band lives.*

We spend countless hours working on intonation, balance, blend, embouchure, posture, articulation, and a host of other technical fundamentals to ensure an excellent performance of the music. Shouldn't we extend those same expectations to the other facets of our band life? It would seem counterproductive to strive for harmonic blend in a beautiful piece of music and not be able to transfer that quality of harmony into the relationships with our fellow band members. We have grown up with constant attention being paid to *proper rehearsal etiquette,* and because of it, we can upgrade the playing level of the rehearsals and the concerts. Why don't we carry those concepts into the other aspects of band? This would likely upgrade the entire band family atmosphere and create a better experience for everyone involved, including *you.*

In many ways, band is an internship for a successful life, and our band community is nothing more than a reflection of the people who make up the ensemble. Therefore, the band will be at the effect of the members' attitudes, moods, personalities, opinions, and a host of traits other than just innate talent. To ignore the feelings of the members, assuming it won't have an impact on the musical artistry, is naive. Music is a language and any fine musician *plays* what he or she feels. That's why we have such an array of musical styles, i.e., blues, classical, marches, overtures, etc.

The music becomes the extension of the person's thoughts and feelings. Undoubtedly, you can remember times when the members were "down" and the rehearsal setting was gloomy and dark; contrary to that situation are the days when everyone is excited and energized and the band seems to play better than ever before. It's true: how your band *lives* has much to do with how your band *plays.*

Learning to deal with musical problems has a direct correlation to learning to deal with life problems, and success in music can often mean more success in life. When the band members can focus their efforts to master a piece of music, it also allows them to see the same kind of cooperative striving can be expanded to generate positive experiences in all facets of life. Ultimately many of the opportunities to enjoy life can best be experienced in a group setting. You sacrifice some of your individuality and, in return, receive the benefits of a musical family. Every band member knows it's the bargain of a lifetime!

So, how does your band live? This poem by Dorothy L. Law really seems to help us understand this important question and goes right to the heart of the matter:

HOW DOES YOUR BAND LIVE?

When the band lives with criticism, they learn to
    condemn.
When the band lives with hostility, they learn to

fight.

When the band lives with fear, they learn to be apprehensive.

When the band lives with pity, they learn to feel sorry for themselves.

When the band lives with ridicule, they learn to be shy.

When the band lives with jealousy, they learn to feel guilty.

When the band lives with encouragement, they learn to be confident.

When the band lives with tolerance, they learn to be patient.

When the band lives with praise, they learn to be appreciative.

When the band lives with acceptance, they learn to love.

When the band lives with fairness, they learn what justice is.

When the band lives with security, they learn to have faith in themselves and those around them.

When the band lives with friendliness, they learn the world is a great place in which to live.

How does your band live?

It's a rather telling bit of poetry, isn't it? Does it provoke some thought for you? It should. We often think that just by rehearsing the music over and over, it will all magically fall into place, but rarely does that happen. Any improvement tends to run parallel with the mood of the band. It certainly could be argued that the band's attitude will improve when the rehearsals and performances get better, but consider the alternative: the rehearsals and performances will improve when the attitudes of the band members improve. Which came first, the chicken or the egg? This age old question will be discussed until the end of time, and the same could be true for the similarity in our band analogy. However, there is one distinctive and important difference: we cannot go back and find the very first chicken...or egg (depending on your opinion), but we *can* have some say-so about the atmosphere created in our bands. More specifically, *you* are in charge of your own attitude, and whatever mood *you* bring to your band class will be evident in the rehearsal.

The next time you walk into the band room, give yourself a quick *attitude check.* What are you bringing to your band family? Look around the room and ask yourself how the response of your fellow band members contributes or distracts from the musical excellence of the ensemble.

Everyone wants to be a valued member of a superior musical organization. This will be accomplished by many hours of dedicated practice, serious study of your instrument, constant listening to quality musicians, and clear focus on the overall atmosphere of the band community. All of these issues play a vital role in the quest for excellence. *How does your band live?*

Playing in the Band

There are many things to do in life,
The choices are quite grand.
But only a musician
Knows how it feels to be in a band.
To share a magical language and create a beautiful sound
The chance to be an artist in a special way, I've found.
My instrument is like a friend
Eager to come out and play.
The more time I spend practicing the better I can say
Those inner thoughts which fill my mind
Beyond the words I speak
Allow me to express myself in a way that's quite unique.
Each day I spend in band
I start to realize
Everything is possible
When seen through music's eyes.
Knowing that bit of wisdom
I now will take a stand,
And pledge myself to excellence
By playing in band.

—Tim Lautzenheiser

"Yes, there is a nirvana; it is leading your sheep to a green pasture, and in putting your child to sleep, and in writing the last line of your poem."
—Kahlil Gibran

About the Author

Tim Lautzenheiser is a well-known name in the music education world as a teacher, clinician, author, composer, consultant, adjudicator, and, above all, a trusted friend to anyone interested in helping young people develop a desire for excellence.

His own career spans ten years of successful college band directing at Northern Michigan University, the University of Missouri, and New Mexico State University. During those years, Tim developed nationally acclaimed groups in all areas of the instrumental and vocal fields. Although every organization from Symphonic Wind Ensemble to Swing Choir was seen as a trend-setter by many of his colleagues, he is best known for his programs dealing with positive attitude, student motivation, and effective leadership training.

After serving three years in the music industry, he created Attitude Concepts for Today, Inc. to meet the many requests he has for workshops, seminars, and convention speaking engagements.

Tim is the author of the best-seller, *The Art of Successful Teaching,* and is a co-author of the popular *Essential Elements* beginning band method.

Tim serves on several of today's educational advisory boards and is also an officer in several professional educational organizations. His work represents a positive blend of realism and idealism, and his tested formula for achieving personal happiness is being successfully proven by many people from coast to coast.